BEYOND THE DICTIONARY
IN FRENCH

CASSELL'S

BEYOND THE DICTIONARY IN FRENCH

by

MICHEL LEVIEUX

Licencié-ès-Lettres, Diplômé d'Etudes
Supérieures de la Sorbonne

and

ELEANOR LEVIEUX, B.A.

FUNK & WAGNALLS
New York

TABLE DES MATIÈRES
TABLE OF CONTENTS

INTRODUCTION	*page* 7
FRENCH–ENGLISH (with commentary)	19
SPECIAL VOCABULARIES	115
La Banque/Banking	115
Faux Amis/False Friends	116
Formules de Politesse/Courtesy	120
Franglais	123
Le Genre/Genders	124
L'Heure/Telling the Time	125
Les Numéros/Numbers	127
Langage Familier/Informal French	128
Le Logement/Housing	132
Le Ménage/The Household	134
La Poste/The Post Office	137
Spectacles/Entertainment	138
Le Téléphone/The Telephone	140
La Voiture/Cars	142
ENGLISH–FRENCH (Cross-reference Index)	145

INTRODUCTION

The scope of this book is, obviously, modest, since we have not aimed at writing a dictionary but at enabling the student with an already solid grounding in French to advance into more secret territory by helping him to read between the lines and fill in the gaps of a standard dictionary. To achieve this, we have attempted to place each of the terms on the following pages IN ITS CONTEXT and, usually, to give examples of its use. A word out of context is virtually useless to you, just another item to chalk up on the vocabulary list. After all, what good is the ace of spades when all the rest of the pack is missing?

When you can wield certain terms deftly, accurately, then you stand an excellent chance of avoiding the more sticky *gaffes* (q.v.) which otherwise fall to the lot of any *étranger*. Which is why we are as likely to stress what not to say—and why—as we are to suggest what you ought to say. We have been especially anxious to point out when a word is used more often than you might suspect on the basis of its twin in English, as with *obligatoire*, for example; and to stress those turns of phrase which are not likely to occur to you the first time you grope for the right expression. *S'occuper de quelque chose* is the proper translation of 'to take care of something', 'to see to something'; whereas you might be tempted to say *prendre soin de quelque chose*—which actually means, 'to take good care of something', that is, 'to be careful of it'.

A word about our choice of words. You may expect to find certain words that do not appear; you may be taken unawares by others that have been included. Our choice has been essentially personal (and therefore, arbitrary), based on the ambushes we have heard English-speaking people run into in France or, conversely, on the stumbling blocks we have known Frenchmen to find most troublesome in learning English. No two persons and certainly no two Franco-Anglo-Saxon (*v.* ANGLO-SAXON) couples would have selected the same terms for your consideration, nor cited the same examples.

We do not pretend to give every meaning of each term, since that would force us straight back to the dictionary form instead of going beyond it; but we have tried to choose some of the meanings which seem to cause the greatest trouble or are likely to be the most useful to you. To this end, we have given some idioms or clichés, although this book is by no means a listing of 'colorful phrases'. Neither is it a handbook of slang, *l'argot*. *Les expressions argotiques* are so many, so peculiar to various *milieux*—and often, so fleeting. *Langage familier*, on the other hand, has not been overlooked, since it is an integral, if not always irreproachable, part of what we aim at helping you use with confidence and understand with ease: the genuine spoken language. In this way, we have included some constructions, some forms which may displease the purists, but whose gradual absorption into modern French is a matter for simple observation. You may rest assured, none the less, that we have not included items of unduly careless, erroneous or undesirable usage. The rare instances of definitely slangy or vulgar language are pointed out as such.

Where we have felt that certain aspects of daily life require, or deserve, a more lingering look, we have grouped the appropriate terms in special categories towards the end of the book; and you will see that they range from banking to theatre-going, from driving a car to telling the time, from telephoning to renting or buying a flat.

You may be shocked at the absence of culinary terms, since France and Food form an indissoluble marriage. But so many competent and even monumental cookbooks do exist already; so many volumes have been, rightfully, devoted to *la cuisine française*; so many guidebooks on what and where to eat in France have been put on the market, that we felt we might make better use of the following pages by devoting them to other things. Which is not to say that you will find no mention whatever of *restaurants*, *cafés*, *casseroles*, *la table*, *le marché*.

Nor is this a manual of grammar. We have taken it for granted that since you are interested enough in French to look into this book, you generally know when a verb is transitive and when it is not. But now and again, where there is an exception or where we foresee confusion, we have indicated the nature of the verb. Again, with adjectives: we have given the feminine form only when it may appear irregular, or to remind you that masculine adjectives in *-eux* take *-euse* in the feminine (*paresseux, -euse,* 'lazy'): that those in *-er* take *-ère* (*gaucher, -ère,* 'left-handed'); those in *-é, -ée,* (*fâché, -ée,* 'angry'); in *-if, -ive* (*compréhensif, -ive,* 'comprehensive' or 'understanding'); in *-nc, -nche* (*blanc, -nche,* 'white'); in *-et, -ète* (*inquiet, -ète,* 'anxious'); and so on.

On the other hand we have, of course, indicated the gender of each noun and called your attention to cases of surprising or double genders.

The plan of the volume as a whole has adhered quite closely to that established in *Beyond the Dictionary in Spanish* (1953) and followed in *Beyond the Dictionary in Italian* (1963). We hope that you will *not* read the book through in one sitting—only to put it away on a shelf, nor resort to it, as a reference book, only in times of stress. Instead, we hope that you will adopt it as a pleasant and very informal guide and companion.

LA PRONONCIATION

PRONUNCIATION

The rules of pronunciation in French are a good deal more stable and less liable to exception than they are in English. The comparative lack of tonal accent is a blessing in this respect: there is little need to look for the accented syllable, even in a word as long as—say—*irrémédiablement*. To an English-speaking person, however, used to doing just that, the relative uniformity of stress in French does not come naturally. (You might note, if it is any comfort to you, a tendency to place a light accent on the last syllable comprising a pronounced vowel: *com/MODE, ci/TERNE*.)

Certainly, you have already realized that English is (and sounds) a more concrete, blunt, synthesizing language than French—which is better adapted to abstract discussions and to analysis, being itself analytically constructed. Diplomats have long appreciated the seeming non-bluntness of French; even insults are attenuated by the time the offending adjective is set off by a *de* here, a *du* there.

Italian is often said to be a very musical language. French is more smooth-flowing and less melodic, but certainly has a definite musicality; and while the English ear can often catch it, the English tongue often finds it impossible to reproduce. Compare a news broadcast on the French radio with one on the BBC or, again, on an American network. We might take one example, more homely and perhaps over-simplified.

The British or American housewife will say, making out her shopping list: 'I need potatoes, French beans, cauliflower, radishes . . .'. And not only will her voice become less audible on the unaccented syllables but also, it will drop a few notes on each comma. Whereas when her French counterpart says *Il me faut des pommes de terre, des haricots verts, un chou-fleur, des radis . . .* , her voice remains even, as regards stress, and rises several notes—expectantly, as it were—at each comma. Hence, schematically, if you will:

po *ta*   French   *cau* li   *rad*
   toes ,   beans ,   flow er ,   ish es . . .

             terre,   verts,   fleur,
des pommes de   des haricots   un chou-
     dis . . .
des ra

To come back to pronunciation *per se*: there is the occasional trap, created by an uncertainty as to how a word is being used; rather like 'read' and 'read' in English. The word *fils* (m. sing.), meaning 'son', rhymes with 'fleece' in English; the word *fils* (m. pl.), meaning 'wires' or 'threads', is pronounced, roughly, 'feel'. (See note below on final *s* and *x*.) And in turn, *un fil*, 'wire' or 'thread', is pronounced like *une file*, 'a line' or 'queue'.

As for the words ending in *-ille*, you had best learn by heart which ones pronounce the double *l*—that is, the minority of them—and which do not. *Une fille* does not, or it would sound like *un fil* and *une file*. But *une ville* does pronounce it, and sounds like *vil*. Some common cases of the silent double *l* are these: *bille, cheville, faucille, fille, gorille, grille, lentille, Manille, morille, quille* ('marble', 'ankle', 'sickle', 'girl', 'gorilla', 'gate', 'lentil', 'Manila', 'type of mushroom', 'keel'). And cases of the audible double *l* are: *Lille, mille, tranquille, ville* ('Lille', 'thousand', 'calm', 'city').

Similarly, a few of the words ending in *-il* make the *l* of that ending inaudible: *fusil, gril, sourcil* ('gun', 'grill', 'eyebrow'); and each of these forms a verb by doubling the *l*, which remains (doubly) silent: *fusiller, griller, sourciller* —'to shoot', 'grill', 'frown'. Whereas *chenil, cil, fil, le Nil*, and *vil* ('kennel', 'eyelash', 'wire', 'the Nile', 'vile') pronounce the *l*. Only two of these latter can form verbs: *filer* ('to spin' or 'run'); and *ciller* ('to blink'), where the double *l* reverts to silence.

Again, the select group of words ending in *-act* or *-ect* seems to cause trouble. Undoubtedly because *un acte* ('act', or 'action') takes an *e* at the end, learners of French, desperate for an analogy, either tack an *e* on to *contact*, *exact*, *infect*, *intact*, *tact* ('contact', 'exact', 'filthy', 'intact', 'tact') even when they are masculine adjectives, or else refuse to pronounce their two final consonants.

Final *s* or *x*—The *s* or *x* which serves to form the plural in French is never pronounced, except when a liaison is required with a vowel or a mute *h* coming immediately after, in which case the *s* or *x* is pronounced with a hard *z* sound: *les avions anglais*, *des gens habiles*, *les beaux arts*. Nor in general do you pronounce a final *s* anywhere, except for deliberate liaison, as in *pas à pas* (paz a pa).[1] The most comical and classic example of an error in this respect is that committed by the person who mispronounces *un corps* ('body'), 'corpse'— suggesting (in English) 'a dead body'! In fact, *corps* is pronounced like *un cor* ('horn'), as in *un cor de chasse*. In words like *un puits* ('a well'), from the Latin *puteus*; *un fonds de commerce* ('good will'), from the Latin *fundus*; and in verb forms like *je prends* ('I take'), the *ts* or *ds* is silent.

The letter *c*—In general, *c* has a hard *k* sound when it occurs in front of *a*, *o*, or *u*—*car*, *colle*, *culot* ('coach', 'glue', 'nerve')—or in front of another consonant.[2]

C can be made soft, and become the *s* sound in front of *a*, *o*, or *u* by the simple addition of *une cédille*: *garçon*, *façade* ('boy', 'façade'). Take the word *macon*, for instance. With a *cédille*, it becomes *un maçon*, 'a mason', and the *c* is pronounced like the *s* in 'mason'. But *Macon*, the name of the town and of the celebrated wine, having no *cédille*, has a *k* sound. The *c* is naturally soft, without need of a *cédille*, when it occurs in front of *e*, *i*, or *y*: *celte*, *cible*, *cynique* ('Celtic', 'target', 'cynical').

The letter *g*—Like *c*, *g* is hard (the *g* of 'guess' in English)

---

[1] Two present-day exceptions which immediately come to mind are *un fils*, as we have seen above, and *un ours*, both of which are pronounced with an audible *s*. Formerly, though, they too abided by the rule of silent *s*.

[2] In English you have two means of arriving at the *k* sound: hard *c*, or *k* itself. In French the number of words beginning with *k* is drastically limited; and those that do exist usually imitate a foreign word starting with hard *c*—*Komintern*, *Krach*—or a foreign word that is virtually international; *kaki*. The *k* sound in French is also arrived at by *qu* in such words as *quartier*, *antiquité* where the *u* is usually silent.

before *a*, *o*, or *u*: *garde, gorge, guttural, gaine, goinfre, goût, guide* ('guard', 'throat', 'guttural', 'girdle', 'guzzler', 'taste', 'guide'). It is soft—pronounced like the *s* in English 'pleasure' or 'leisure'—before *e* or *i*, or *y*: *genou, gifle, gynécologie* ('knee', 'slap', 'gynæcology'). *G* is never pronounced like the English soft *g* or the English *j*, as in 'George', 'gesture', 'John', 'judge'. The combination *gn*, as in *ignorer, guignol* is generally pronounced like *ny* in front of a vowel; that is, like the Spanish *ñ*. But in words of Greek origin, like *agnostique*, you pronounce hard *g* and *n*.

The letter *j* is never pronounced like *j* in the English 'judge', but like the French soft *g* (the *s* in English 'pleasure'): *Jean, juge, jauge* ('John', 'judge', 'gauge').

The combination *ch* is pronounced like the English *sh*, as in *chute*; or, in some words of Greek origin, like *k*: *psychiatre*.

And by the way, in words such as *psychiatre, psaume* ('psychiatrist', 'psalm') the *p* is pronounced as well as the *s*. Similarly, in *pneumatique*, you pronounce both the *p* and the *n*.

Initial *d* and initial *t* form one of the subtler indices which reveal whether a speaker is French, or a foreigner speaking good French. The difference is that in English, you attack these initial consonants, whereas in French you slide up to them. 'Tea' is palatal and explosive; *le thé* is dental and softer. Similarly, initial *p* is softer in French.

QUELQUES COMMENTAIRES

MISCELLANEOUS NOTES

Possession—It is worth reminding yourself that the possessive pronoun and adjective agree in number and in gender with the thing possessed, and not, as is the case in English, with the possessor. In English, you say 'his beard'; in French, *sa barbe*, or *la sienne* ('his'), since the word for 'beard' is feminine in French. Or again, 'her handbag' becomes *son sac à main*, and *le sien* ('hers'). The plural in either case is expressed by *ses*: *sa plume, ses plumes* ('his *or* her pen', 'his *or* her pens'); *son pied, ses pieds* ('his or her foot', 'his *or* her feet'). In other words, the possessive pronoun or adjective tells you only about the thing(s) possessed; you need the entire context in order to know who possesses the thing in question.

For the sake of euphony, you will say *son* (*mon, ton*) *aventure*, although the word is feminine, simply to avoid the head-on collision of two vowels which would occur if you said *sa aventure, ma eau, ta oreille*.

A word on *les adjectifs substantivés*—In English we find adjectives made into COLLECTIVE nouns only when they denote animate things: 'the rich', 'the poor', 'the guilty', 'the wounded'. In French, however, this technique is used in the singular and for inanimate things too: *le coupable, l'intéressé, le blessé*. Notice that when translating such transformed adjectives into English, you have to use an adjective plus a (pro)noun: 'the guilty one', 'the interested party' (or 'the person concerned'), 'the wounded man'. Further and very common examples are: *Je ferai le nécessaire*: 'I shall take the necessary steps'; and *Il a fait son possible* (or *l'impossible*): 'He did all he could, all that was humanly possible'.

Adjectives—Many of the more colloquial and vivid adjectives are present participles. For instance: *agaçant*, 'annoying' or 'irritating'; *crevant*, 'deadly tiring' or 'killing' ('funny'); *embêtant*, 'irksome' or 'boring'; *empoisonnant* is similar to *embêtant* but is stronger, meaning 'a dreadful nuisance'; *enquiquinant* is similar to *empoisonnant*; *épatant*, 'marvellous' (a bit out-dated now and replaced by *formidable* etc.); *époustouflant*, like *étonnant*, means 'astonishing'; *exigeant*, 'demanding'; *tordant*, although its literal meaning is 'twisting', is extended to mean 'killingly funny'.

There are, however, numerous examples to prove that this is not necessarily so. 'Boring', for instance, is not '*ennuyant*', as you might expect, but *ennuyeux*.

Certain other adjectives may suprise you. In some cases, the corresponding expression in English is stronger, or rarer, or is used differently, or is longer.

> *affreux*—'frightful', i.e. 'awful' (dress, experience etc.)
> *exécrable*—'terrible', 'extremely bad' (*une soirée*, or *un goût exécrable*)
> *fatal*—'mortal', 'deadly'; but also and especially, 'fated', 'predestined'
> *formidable*—'stunning', 'marvellous'
> *inadmissible*—'unacceptable', 'not to be stood for'
> *inouï*—'unheard of'
> *insolite*—'original', 'startling', 'unexpected'
> *insupportable*—'unbearable'
> *invivable*—'impossible to live with', 'unbearable'
> *moche*—'homely', 'shabby', 'dowdy'; 'bad luck'; the opposite of 'glamorous'
> *mortel*—'mortal', 'fatal' (wound); but also, 'deadly boring'
> *terrible*—'terrible', *terrifiant*; but also a compliment: 'stunning', 'forceful', 'with lots of personality', 'a wow'

For more adjectives (and other words) which may catch you off balance, see FAUX-AMIS at the end of the book.

Some adverbs, too, may need cautious handling. *Joliment*, for instance, on the face of it means 'prettily'—and so it does; but it can also be used like *rudement* (see below) and the more colloquial *bigrement*, to mean 'awfully', 'dreadfully': *Cette pièce est joliment sale.* 'This is an awfully dirty room'.

Drôlement is another case in point. It does indeed mean

'funnily', 'drolly'; but again, 'awfully', 'terribly': *C'est drôlement loin.* 'It's really awfully far away'.

Or again, *rudement* and *méchamment*: 'rudely', 'nastily', but also, 'awfully'. *L'examen était méchamment dur.* 'The exam was terribly tough'.

Suffixes and prefixes all, of course, require careful attention. For example, suffixes such as *-ard*, *-aille(r)* and *-ouille(r)* instantly transform a perfectly sober word into a much more colloquial one, often near slang, and/or with a derogatory tinge. *Un chauffeur*, 'driver'; *un chauffard*, 'reckless driver'. *Une pantoufle*, 'slipper'; *un pantouflard*, 'a stay-at-home'. *Un moteur*, 'motor'; *un motard*, 'motorcycle policeman'. *Une veine*, 'luck'; *un veinard*, 'lucky chap'.

Tripoter, 'to finger', 'tinker *or* tamper with'; *tripatouiller*, 'to do this exaggeratedly'.

The suffix *-oter* diminishes the quality of the verb: *vivre*, 'to live'; *vivoter*, 'to live skimpily', 'to struggle along'. *Dormir*, 'to sleep'; *dormoter*, 'to snooze fitfully'.

So do *-acher* and *-icher*, in a more mocking way. *Tomber amoureux de*, 'to fall in love with'; *s'amouracher de*, 'to be infatuated with'.

The superlative *-issime* is easy to overdo: *riche*, rich; *richissime*, ultra rich.

The prefix *archi-* acts the same way, as a prefix, and is much affected by students.

The principal negative prefixes are *non-* and *im-* or *in-* (*im-* before a *b* or a *p*, as *imbuvable*, *impensable*: 'undrinkable', 'unthinkable'; *in-* elsewhere, as *incohérent*, *indécent*, *injuste*: 'incoherent', 'indecent', 'unjust'). The negative prefix *un-*, so common in English, is not found in French.

A

abordable. This means 'approachable', 'within reach', and applies particularly to prices. *Les fraises sont inabordables en cette saison.* 'Strawberries are sky-high at this time of year.'

Aborder means 'to approach', a shore or a person, and here *abordable* would mean 'approachable', 'amiable in aspect'. *Certains de nos voisins sont peu abordables.* 'Some of our neighbors are not very friendly.' You are of course familiar with *d'abord*, 'first of all'; and with *de prime abord*, 'at first glance'. And whereas *par dessus bord* does mean 'overboard', 'All aboard!' must be translated by *Messieurs, Dames en voiture.*[1]

abruti. A very common adjective, often taken as a noun, from the verb *abrutir*, meaning 'to daze' or 'make stupid'. The adjective has a distinctly pejorative tinge when applied to someone else —*Espèce d'abruti!* 'Blockhead!' 'You dope!' —but you can apply it in all innocence to yourself: *Au bout de cinq heures de travail d'une traite, je suis totalement abruti.* 'After working five hours at a stretch, I'm in a real fog, I feel washed out.' The work itself could be called *abrutissant.*

accord (m). Roughly, any sort of agreement or harmony, from cultural to grammatical. *D'accord*, perhaps less desirable than *entendu* or *c'est entendu*, is the commonest way of saying, 'all right', 'OK.' *Je suis d'accord avec lui.* 'I agree with him.'

affaire (f). 'A bargain.' *Faire une (bonne) affaire*, 'to make a bargain'. *Faire une mauvaise affaire*, 'to make a bad bargain'.

'An affair', 'a matter': *Il m'a longuement entretenu de toute l'affaire.* 'He spoke to me at length about the whole matter.'

You will recall that in the plural, *affaires* means '(big) business', as in *un homme d'affaires*, 'a businessman'.—*Comment vont les affaires?—Plutôt bien.* 'How's business?—Pretty good.' An *affairiste* is an 'unscrupulous businessman'. *Les affaires* can also be one's 'belongings'. (*v.* JUSTE.)

The meaning of *s'affairer* (*autour de quelque chose ou de quelqu'un*) goes off on a slight tangent: 'to bustle about.'

The English term, 'an affair', or 'a love affair', is translated by *liaison* (f). *Une affaire de cœur* is simply 'a matter of the heart'.

---

[1] Strictly speaking, the stationmaster (*le chef de gare*) should say 'Mesdames, Mesdemoiselles, Messieurs', but in practice, hardly anyone but lecturers, or announcers on the radio, will be so formal.

afficher. A transitive verb, meaning 'to post notices' (*une affiche*). *Défense d'Afficher Loi du 29 Juillet 1881* ('Billposting forbidden by the law of 29 July 1881') is still to be found in big black letters on countless walls in Paris.

Afficher, in a more *familier* usage, means 'to flaunt', 'show off': *Elle n'hésite pas à s'afficher partout avec ce type-là.* 'She is quite shameless about going around everywhere with that fellow.'

affranchir. First of all, 'to free', 'to liberate'. *La question de l'affranchissement des esclaves fut à la base du conflit.* 'The issue of emancipation for the slaves was one of the root causes of the war.' It is encountered more frequently in the sense of 'paying postage' on a letter or package. *Une carte pour l'Italie est affranchie à vingt-cinq.* 'A post card to Italy needs a 25 centime stamp.'

S'affranchir sur quelque chose or *être affranchi sur quelque chose* is a slangy way of saying *se mettre (être) au courant*: 'to be up to date'. It follows that *affranchir quelqu'un sur quelque chose* means 'to bring someone up to date on something'.

agrandir. 'To enlarge'. *Un agrandissement* is any sort of enlargement. This is the word you need when you bring in negatives to the photographer's to have them blown up: *Je voudrais trois agrandissements de chaque négatif, 18 sur 24.* 'Will you please make three enlargements of each negative, 7 by 10 inches.' [By the way, it is well to remember that 'the photographer' is *le photographe*, whereas 'the photograph' or 'the art of photography' is *la photo(graphie)*.]

En faisant reculer cette cloison j'ai pu agrandir mon salon. 'By having this partition moved back, I was able to make my living room bigger.'

agréer. Not really 'to agree' (v. ACCORD) but 'to approve', 'grant', 'accept'. *Agréer une demande*, 'to grant a request' or 'act favorably upon an application'. *Agrément* (m) therefore is either 'consent' or, more often, 'pleasure' (*un jardin d'agrément*, 'pleasure garden'), but rarely 'agreement'.

Aïe! 'Ow!' 'Ouch!' 'That hurts!'

aimant (m). 'A magnet.' And the verb is either *aimanter* or *magnétiser*. *Magnétiser* (or *hypnotiser*) *quelqu'un* means 'to hypnotize someone'.

air (m). Included here to remind you how useful *avoir l'air* can be as a way of avoiding *sembler*, *paraître*. 'He looked tired.' *Il avait l'air fatigué.* 'She would seem to be wealthy.' *Elle a l'air d'être riche.*

aller. *allez, allons, va!* As you can see, we want to stress the exclamatory uses of this verb, which, just like 'go' in English, lends itself to a whole list of expressions. Depending on the tone of voice, *allez!* can mean encouragement or derision:

'come on!' or else, 'go on!', 'come off it!' and so on. *Allons allons,
soyons raisonnables*: 'Come on now, let's not overdo it!'—or
any number of translations, depending on the context. *Va!*,
especially, may be said to equate with 'there!' when it comes
at the end of a sentence: *Ah, ne te fâche pas, va!*, or *Bon, fais
ce que tu voudras, va!* The tone here is conciliatory or soothing.

aller (m). When buying a travel ticket, you specify *un aller-retour*,
which is 'a return ticket' (US: 'round trip') or, *un aller
simple*, 'a single (*or* one-way) ticket'.

allonger. You might take especial note of the culinary aspect of
this word. *Allonger une sauce* means 'to stretch a sauce by
thinning it'.

ampoule (f). A word which you'll find in several contexts. *Une
ampoule au talon* is 'a blister on your heel'. But when the
doctor prescribes *une ampoule matin et soir* for stomach
trouble, you are to drink 'a tube-full of liquid medicine twice
a day'. The transparent *ampoule* is now an exceedingly common way of packaging medicines in France, and you have to
be careful not to saw off the two ends of it into the glass from
which you're going to drink it! There are *ampoules injectables*
(for injections or rectal use) as well as *ampoules buvables*. And
of course there is the *ampoule électrique*, the 'electric light bulb',
which you buy *chez le marchand de couleurs* or *le droguiste*. If
you're looking for a 'standard (US: floor) lamp', stand and all,
you mean *un lampadaire*; 'a chandelier' is *un lustre*. Be careful:
un chandelier in French means 'a branched candlestick'; a plain
one is *un bougeoir*. *Une lampe* is 'a table lamp'; *une lampe de
poche* or *lampe électrique*, 'an electric torch' (US: 'flashlight').
And 'a wall lamp' or 'sconce' is *une applique*. Conveniently
enough, 'a candelabra' is *un candélabre*.

amuse-gueule (m). Usually used in the plural, *amuse-gueules*: the
various salty or savory things that accompany cocktails. A
perfectly acceptable term, though *gueule* (f) by itself is a vulgar
term for 'face'.

anglo-saxon. Loosely extended to mean 'English-speaking', as
in *les pays anglo-saxons*.

anticipation (f). Often used synonymously with *la science-fiction*:
un roman d'anticipation.

antiquité (f). In the singular, the word means 'ancient times',
'classical times', 'antiquity'. *Il se prend pour un héros de l'Antiquité.* 'He thinks he's one of the epic heroes of ancient Greece.'
In the plural, it means 'antiques', and you will see *antiquités*
or *objets anciens* written above antique dealers' shops. The
dealer himself is *l'antiquaire*.

appareil (m). Literally any apparatus, any machine. *On vient d'in-
venter un appareil génial pour les plongées en grande profondeur.*
'They've just invented an ingenious machine for the purpose

of depth diving.' Most often, this will mean 'the telephone'. *Attention, tu as laissé l'appareil décroché.* 'Be careful, you left the phone off the hook.' (v. TÉLÉPHONE.)

Or again, it may mean 'a camera': *un appareil photo.* Be careful of the word *caméra* (f) in French: it means only a 'motion-picture camera' and so is likely to be something of a *Faux Ami* for you.

appel (m). From *appeler*, of course, 'to call' or 'name'. Particular note should be taken of *appel téléphonique*, meaning 'a call' especially from the point of view of the person being called, or in official language, as when you telephone from the post office. *Communication* (f) would be the term more likely used by the person calling.

Faire appel à (*la bonté de quelqu'un*) is 'to appeal to', 'to call upon'. *Lancer un appel* is 'to launch an appeal', in the sense of a campaign. The English 'to appeal' can have as many different translations as there are contexts: *plaire, séduire, tenter, attirer, être attachant,* even *dire*. 'Let's not go to see that film; it doesn't appeal to me.' *Ce film-là ne me dit rien; n'allons pas le voir.* 'The little puppy looked at me so appealingly I just had to buy him.' *Le petit chiot avait un regard si attachant que ça a été plus fort que moi: je l'ai acheté.*

And of course there is *appellation contrôlée*, or 'registered trade name', essential to the vocabulary of all wine *connaisseurs*.

appoint (m). *Faire l'appoint*, 'to have the exact change'. A notice in the bus will read: *Vous êtes priés de faire l'appoint.* 'Please get the right change ready.'

appointements (m. pl.). Another but less common term for *salaire* (m). *Ses appointements ne sont pas très élevés mais il a aussi des avantages en nature.* 'His pay isn't much but he also has some compensations in kind.' *Le salaire* is 'salary'; if you mean 'wages', then you say *gages* (m. pl.), which has the general meaning of 'hire', as well: *un tueur à gages*, 'a hired gunman'. *Honoraires* (m. pl.) are 'non-regular payments or fees': what you pay *l'avocat, le dentiste, le docteur, le conférencier, le traducteur,* and so on. Also, in speaking of medical care, you can simply say *je paie tant la visite* (either your visits to the practitioner's office or his visits *à domicile*) or *tant les soins.* A payment on a car or anything else bought *à crédit* is *un versement.* 'The deposit' which you leave in the beginning is called *les arrhes. Pour mon nouveau poste de télévision, j'ai versé 300 francs d'arrhes, et le solde en 4 versements trimestriels.* 'I paid 300 francs down on my new TV set and the rest in 4 quarterly payments.'

Soldes (m. pl.) is the term for 'clearance sales', while *solde* (f) means 'military pay'. (*v.* also AVOIR).

appuyer. Used in a way which the ladies may encounter when they go to buy a dress: *une robe légèrement appuyée à la taille* is 'a dress slightly indented at, marking, the waist'.

S'appuyer une tâche ou une corvée is a very colloquial way of saying 'to have to do some disagreeable task *or* drudgery'.

après-ski (m. pl.). *Les après-ski*, in spite of their name, are just as often worn in town, and generally by children or older boys in school. They are simply heavy ankle-high shoes, a bit inaesthetic as a rule but warm and waterproof, and often with the furside outside, as Hiawatha would say.

arête (f). 'A fish bone'; never called *un os*, which is the bone of anything but fish.

armoire à glace (f). Since this means 'a wardrobe', you may be puzzled the first time you hear a man described as *une véritable armoire à glace*: yet this is an almost standard way of saying that the person is very big and strong, square built.

arranger. 'To arrange', of course, but much more often 'to fix', 'patch up', 'improve', 'decorate', 'repair'. *Son studio est gentiment arrangé.* 'His (one-room) flat is fixed up handsomely'. *Laissez donc, je vais arranger ça.* 'Never mind, I'll take care of that.'

Special note should be taken of *arrangeant(e)* and *arrangement* (m). The adjective is almost akin to *serviable* (q.v.) and means the opposite of 'fussy' or 'uncooperative', that is, 'accommodating', 'helpful'. *Il s'est montré vraiment très arrangeant.* 'He proved really most cooperative.' And while *un arrangement* can be a musical one, done by *un arrangeur*, very often it is an understanding between two parties, and the expression *un arrangement à l'amiable* is quite common—thank goodness: it means 'a civilized settlement of a dispute, without going to court'. *L'autre conducteur a consenti à un arrangement à l'amiable.*

arrêté (m). *Un arrêté préfectoral, ministériel,* etc. is 'a decree', for which another and less surprising word is, roughly speaking, *un décret* or *un décret-loi.*

arrhes (f. pl.). This is the deposit which you pay down on something you are buying on short- or long-term credit. (*v.* VERSER). But the deposit you pay on a bottle or a jar is *la consigne* (q.v.).

arriver. 'To arrive', 'to come', of course, in the literal sense. But when *quelque chose arrive à quelqu'un*, the meaning is 'to happen'. 'A funny thing happened to me on the way to the office' would be *il m'est arrivé un drôle de truc* (or *quelque chose de bizarre) en allant au bureau. Malgré son grand âge, il lui arrive encore de faire cinq km à pied.* 'Old as he is, none the less he sometimes walks five kilometres.'

'To manage' may be another meaning, as in *Je n'arrive pas à fermer les volets.* 'I can't manage to get the shutters closed.'

Qu'est-ce qui vous arrive? may often mean *qu'avez-vous?*, 'what's happened?' 'what's the matter?'

When someone rings your doorbell, you say '(I'm) coming'. The Frenchman, however, does not say *je viens*, but *j'arrive*. Most especially, the garçon at the *café, terrasse*, or *restaurant* where you have seated yourself will call *j'arrive!* from somewhere in the depths of the establishment to assure you that your presence has not gone unnoticed.

Un arriviste is *un ambitieux*, often unscrupulous and always unabashed about his determination to make his way up the social ladder; the science is *l'arrivisme*.

Arrivée (f) at the railway station or the airport means simply 'Arrivals', as opposed to *Départ* (m), 'Departures'.

Un arrivage is 'a delivery' of vegetables, fruit, or fish.

arrondir. Comparable to the meaning of *allonger* (q.v.) which we have stressed, but without the culinary context. *Il donne des petits cours pour arrondir son mois.* 'He gives private lessons to eke out his income.' *Arrondir les angles*, 'to be conciliatory', 'avoid arguments', 'have a softening influence'.

arroser. 'To water', as plants, with *un arrosoir* ('watering can'). A more colloquial meaning is, literally, 'to wine'!—'to celebrate with a good bottle'. *Mais c'est une nouvelle merveilleuse! Ça s'arrose!* 'That's splendid news! We must celebrate!'

Un café arrosé is a coffee into which you have poured some cognac or calvados.

And to distribute tips lavishly, give handouts, is also *arroser*.

article (m). Any 'article', grammatical, journalistic, or other. But you should be careful of the special and restrictive meaning of *articles de Paris*, written over shops selling small luxury items which represent the traditional French *'chic'* and elegance, *les petits riens* which can transform a staid suit or a dull dress; hence, gloves, lace, perfumes, scarves and so on.

And when you hear that someone is *à l'article de la mort*, you should know that he is 'at death's door.'

Faire l'article pour quelque chose is a faintly pejorative expression, implying a certain amount of *boniment* (q.v.) and meaning 'to give a high-pressure sales talk for the thing (*or* person) in question', 'to vaunt' its qualities. *Mais oui, mon vieux, inutile de me faire l'article pour ton tournevis perfectionné, je le connais déjà.* 'It's all right, old man, I know all about your perfected screwdriver, you don't have to convince me.'

artisanat (m). The work done by *un artisan*, the self-employed individual craftsman; or the class of such craftsmen. *L'artisanat se perd*, as people often moan today: 'individual craftsmanship is harder and harder to find'.

ascenseur (m). 'The lift' (US: 'elevator'), as you know; but we would like to remind you that in many older buildings it lives up to its name, since you are supposed to use it only for going up but not for going down. You press the button and send it down empty to the main floor for the convenience of the next person. Frustrating but, surprisingly enough, a rule which people generally abide by.

asparagus (m). If you ask for *asparagus* at the greengrocer's (*le marchand de primeurs* or *le marchand des quatre saisons*), you may receive a strange look and be sent next door to *le fleuriste*, because this is the word for the 'ferns' (actually, 'asparagus leaves') which accompany a bouquet. If you want simple greenery with your *tulipes*, you ask for *un peu de feuillage*. And if you really want 'asparagus', the vegetable, then it's *asperges* (q.v.) you're looking for.

asperge (f). 'Asparagus', the vegetable. (*v.* ASPARAGUS). *Je ne mange pas souvent d'asperges*. 'I don't often eat asparagus' (note the plural in French).

Asperger means 'to sprinkle' or 'splash'.

assez. A word that bears looking at from more than one angle. It means 'enough': *il y en a assez*, 'there's enough of it'. *Il gagne assez*. 'He earns enough.' But it also means 'fairly' or 'rather' and *il gagne assez bien*, 'he earns a fair amount (rather well)', does not necessarily mean the same as *il gagne assez*.

In the sense of quantity ('rather'), *assez* can be replaced by *plutôt*: *elle est plutôt jolie*. But if you mean quality or preference then *assez* will not do. *Elle est plutôt jolie que laide*. 'She's rather pretty than ugly'.

En avoir assez de quelque chose is, literally, 'to have enough of something', 'to be fed up with it'. *En avoir marre* is an inelegant way of saying the same thing, common enough, heaven knows.

astuce (f). The dictionary meaning is limited to 'craft', 'ruse'. But in actual daily use, the meaning is extended to 'the tricky thing to do', 'the way out', 'the solution'. *Une simple astuce suffit pour résoudre ce problème*. 'All you need, to solve this problem, is to know a simple trick.'—*Je n'y arrive pas.— Question d'astuce!* 'I can't do it'—'Find the gimmick!'

Une astuce is also a 'clever play on words'.

Astucieux, meaning 'clever' or 'inventive', can be applied to things or to persons. *C'est très astucieux, cette chaise qui se replie.* 'That folding chair is ingenious.' *Ma couturière est vraiment astucieuse: elle a de ces trouvailles même pour mes vieilles robes démodées!* 'My dressmaker is so clever; she has such marvellous ideas even for my old dresses that have gone out of fashion!'

attenant. 'Adjoining', 'communicating', as two rooms or two houses.

attirer. 'To attract', i.e. 'to draw', without necessarily being attractive (*v.* ATTRAYANT). *Il a attiré mon attention sur cette* *vieille maison, fort attrayante.* 'He drew my attention to that very attractive old house.' *Ce tissu attire la poussière.* 'This cloth attracts dust.'

attrayant. 'Attractive'; rarely found in the form of the archaic infinitive, *attraire*, which can also be avoided by the use of the noun, *attrait* (m). *La montagne a un attrait irrésistible pour moi.* 'The mountains have an irresistible attraction for me.' 'To attract attention' requires *attirer* (q.v.).

auberge (f). 'An inn' or 'hostel' (a youth hostel is *une auberge de jeunesse,* or *AJ*); also, a name much affected by restaurants which deliberately set out to be quaint or old-fashioned. More likely than not, they will call themselves *l'Auberge du Cheval Blanc* or *du Coq d'Or.*

You might pay particular attention to *pas encore sorti de l'auberge,* a colloquial expression which, surprisingly enough, means 'not yet out of hot water', 'still in trouble'. *Avec un pneu crevé, ils ne sont pas encore sortis de l'auberge.* 'They're in a real fix with that flat tire.'

au-delà. 'Beyond'; the opposite is *en-deçà. L'au-delà* is 'the beyond', hence, 'the next life' and contrasts with *ici-bas,* 'here below', hence, 'this life on earth.'

au diable. Used by itself, this gives the idea of excessive distance. *Vous n'allez pas jusque là pour lui rendre son livre? C'est au diable (vauvert).* 'You're not going all the way there just to give him back his book! It's at the end of the earth.'

Aller au diable is something else again. *Si ce type t'embête encore, tu n'as qu'à lui dire d'aller au diable.* 'If that fellow bothers you again, just tell him where to go (to go to the devil).'

And *faire quelque chose à la diable,* 'to do something carelessly, any old way'.

aussi. You are familiar with the meaning of 'too', 'also'. But for that reason, you may sometimes be tripped up by a different meaning, appearing at the start of a sentence or phrase and usually requiring an inverted verb-subject order afterwards: 'therefore', 'in accordance' (with what has just preceded). *Sa famille s'en va, aussi doit-il la suivre.* 'Since his family is going away, he (accordingly) has to follow them.'

autrement. 'Otherwise', '(or) else', when used with a verb. *Fais vite, autrement je terminerai avant toi.* 'Hurry up, or else I'll finish before you do.'

'Much more', or 'very', when used with an adjective, especially in comparisons. *Cet examen était autrement plus difficile que le premier.* 'This exam was a much tougher job than the first'.

Autrement dit, 'in other words'.

avec. Colloquially, the prepositions *avec* and *sans* are used in an adjectival or adverbial sense. During the Second World War, *les jours avec et les jours sans* referred to the days with or without meat, sugar, and so on. *Ayant acheté un nouveau disque, il est venu avec.* 'He'd got a new record and brought it along.'

avenant (m). Most commonly heard in the expression, *et tout à l'avenant*, 'and so on', 'in the same way', 'similarly'. *Ces gens-là aiment le faux partout, des bustes 'anciens', guéridons 'Louis XV', et tout à l'avenant.* 'People like that go in for fake this and imitation that everywhere, "antique" busts, little "Louis XV" tables, and so on, straight down the line.'

    Ajouter un avenant is 'to add a clause or a rider to a contract'.

avoir (m). *Un avoir* is a sum with which you are credited. If you pay up at the grocer's at the end of the month with a 100 fr. note because you've nothing smaller, then you may have some *avoir* for the next month. Once you have paid down a deposit on a purchase (*v.* ARRHES), this deposit can be considered your *avoir*, as opposed to *le solde*, the sum which remains to be paid.

    Se faire avoir (or *se faire rouler*) is a sad little phrase, meaning 'to be taken in' *or* 'for a ride', 'to be had'. It follows of course that *avoir quelqu'un* means 'to get the better of someone', 'to take him for a ride'; and you can use it in teasing: *ah, je vous ai eu, hein?* 'You see, I fooled you, didn't I?'

B

bacon (m). No trouble in understanding here; but it is pronounced with some stress on the second syllable, thus: *bay-KUN*.

bagage (m). Two things which you can never notice too often about this word are: the spelling, and the fact that it is generally used in the plural, *les bagages*, when given the tangible sense of suitcases, trunks and what not. If you want it to mean 'mental equipment', one's 'stock of knowledge', then you revert to the singular. *Il faut que j'aille demain dédouaner mes bagages.* 'Tomorrow I'll have to put my luggage through customs.' *Dans ce domaine-là il a un bagage considérable.* 'He's very knowledgeable in that field.'

baigneur (m). 'A bather', of course; and particularly the sort of small flesh-colored rubber or plastic doll clearly resembling the infant who will undress it and drag it into his bath with him.

banlieue (f). 'The suburbs'; and you may distinguish between *la proche banlieue*, 'the nearer *or* immediate suburbs', and *la* *grande banlieue*, 'the outlying ones'. *Un banlieusard* is the suburbanite who commutes via *le train de banlieue*.

baratin or **barattin** (m). Like *boniment* (q.v.), quite *familier*, but minus the implication of making an effort to sell. It means 'hot air', 'loose, inconsequential talk', 'a spiel'. *Quand il s'agit de baratiner, il n'a pas son égal.* 'When it comes to giving you a long spiel, there's nobody like him.' A young man, in order to catch a girl's interest, will become a *baratineur* and follow her along.

barrage (m). 'A roadblock.' *Sur la route de Senlis, nous avons été retardés par un barrage de gendarmerie.* 'We were delayed on our way to Senlis by a roadblock the police had set up.' Another way of expressing the same thing is to say *la route était barrée*.

Or again, 'a dam'. *Le nouveau barrage a créé un joli lac.* 'The new dam has created a pretty lake.'

bassin (m). With **bassine** (f), this word seems to form one of those pairs which people have trouble keeping straightened out, like *la paillasse* ('straw mattress' or 'drain board of a sink') and *le paillasson* ('doormat'). *Un bassin* is *une pièce d'eau*: 'a pool' or 'pond'; whereas the humble *bassine* is *une cuvette*, or 'wash-basin'.

bémol (m). 'Flat', not in the sense of a lodging, but in music. 'A sharp' is *un dièse*. The English musical scale is, in French, Do Ré Mi Fa Sol La Si Do (C D E F G A B C). *Majeur* and *mineur* are certainly obvious, except in so far as *majeur* also means 'of legal age', and as *mineur* may signify 'under legal age' or, when a masculine noun, 'a miner'.

bénéfice (m). 'Benefit', but also, just as often, 'profit'. A word which learners of French seem reluctant to use: perhaps it looks or sounds too feminine. Something of a *Faux Ami*.

bêtise (f). Any mother of very young children is bound to use this word at least once a day: *Tu ne fais que des bêtises!* 'You're always getting into trouble, doing something you shouldn't.' But adults can say it just as well of themselves or other adults: *J'ai fait une bêtise* could often be translated 'I could kick myself!' In which case you may find *des Bêtises de Cambrai* soothing—rather sharp mints.

bibelot (m). Any small (decorative) object, trinket, gewgaw, usually useless, sometimes antique (*bibelots anciens*), and collected or offered as a gift. The word takes on a slightly derisive tinge when used by someone who doesn't go in for such things.

bic (m). 'A ball-point pen'. Originally a trade name, the word has become identified with the article itself, whatever its make, just as in the case of *un Kodak* and *un Frigidaire*.

billet (m). 'A note'; 'a bank note'; and the normal word for a 'travel *or* theatre ticket'. *Un ticket* does exist, but applies only to municipal bus or Paris Métro tickets, and to meal tickets at student restaurants. Or again, *un ticket de quai*, without which you cannot go farther than the waiting room of a railway station when you've come to see someone off or to meet a train.

billion (m). No longer means what 'billion' still means in the United States, i.e. 'a thousand millions'; this is expressed by *milliard* (m). No, since 1948 *un billion* has meant, as in the U.K., 'a million millions': 1,000,000,000,000. *Un billion* is more commonly called *mille milliards*.

blague (f). 'A joke'; a more colloquial term than *une plaisanterie*, and usually a less verbal sort of joke. *Blague à part* (or to be still more *familier*), *blague dans le coin*, means 'no kidding', 'no joke', 'seriously'. *Sans blague!* would be your answer to someone else's startling statement.
    Pipe smokers should know that *une blague à tabac* is 'a tobacco pouch'.

bleu (m). 'A black-and-blue mark' or 'bruise'; or again, 'a work-man's overalls' (*v.* COMBINAISON), *un bleu de travail*.
    Also, 'blue cheese': *le bleu d'Auvergne, le bleu des Causses*.
    'To feel *or* be blue', or 'to have the blues' is *avoir le cafard* or *être cafardeux*. But the blues in jazz are never called *les cafards!*, nor *les bleus*: simply *les blues* (pronounced 'blooze').
    Speaking of colors, there is a whole palette of expressions, such as *être noir*, 'to be drunk', 'half-seas over'.
    être marron: se faire avoir, 'to be taken in'.
    un avocat marron: 'a dishonest lawyer'.
    un jaune: 'a strikebreaker'.
    le maillot jaune: 'the leading cyclist in the Tour de France'.
    le gros rouge (qui tache): 'ordinary cheap wine'.
    se mettre au vert: se reposer à la campagne, 'to relax in the country'.
    être blanc comme un linge: 'to be white as a sheet'.
    v. also: COULEURS.

blouson noir (m). A term which, unhappily, is likely to become familiar to you even after a brief perusal of *les journaux*: this is the French equivalent of the 'juvenile delinquent' and he is named after his black leather jacket. An extension of this, *le blouson doré*, refers to a *fils à papa*, or 'spoiled rich boy', who goes to the bad.

bobo. The baby word for 'hurt', 'pain'. *Où as-tu bobo?* 'Where does it hurt you?' *Mais non, n'aie pas peur, ça ne fait pas bobo.* 'Don't be afraid, it doesn't hurt.' (Even adults may sometimes say *il n'y a pas de bobo*, a very informal substitute for *il n'y a pas de mal*: 'there's no harm done, nothing serious.')
    There is of course an infinity of baby words built on the same double-syllable principle. *Lolo, le lait; nounou, la nurse*

or *la gouvernante*; *nounours, l'ours en peluche*, 'teddy bear';
dodo, le sommeil. Fais un gros dodo, 'sleep tight'.

boisson (f). The general word for 'beverage', 'drink'. If you want
a drink (of something alcoholic, especially), you had best say *je
voudrais un verre de* . . . or, if you're really up on your Franglais,
un drink. On the menu, *boisson en plus* (or *en sus*) warns you
that your beverage is not included in the price of the meal.
Once you have ordered your main dish, *le garçon* or *la serveuse*
will ask *et comme boisson, s'il vous plaît?* 'And what will you
have to drink?' The choice will be between wine and mineral
water, or possibly beer; you must not expect a request for
coffee or tea *with* the meal to be heard with equanimity. . . .
In other contexts, *la boisson* and *boire* can, just like drink in
English, refer specifically to alcohol. *Il boit un peu trop*, 'he
drinks a bit too much'. *Quand je l'ai vu hier soir, il était pris
de boisson.* 'When I saw him last night, he was drunk.' *Être
porté sur la boisson*, 'to be given to drink'.

boîte (f). Any sort of box, from *boîte de conserve*, 'can of food', to
boîte aux lettres. Mettre une lettre à la boîte, 'to mail a letter',
'put it in the pillarbox' (US: 'mailbox'), as distinct from
mettre une lettre à la poste, 'to take a letter to the post office'.
Une grosse boîte is a familiar term for *une grosse maison*, 'a
big or important business firm'.
But *une boîte (de nuit)* is 'a night club'.
La boîte à ordures is the individual garbage pail or dust-bin
which you empty into the collective *poubelle* (f) of your building each evening. The dustman or trash collector is *l'éboueur*.
Mettre quelqu'un en boîte, 'to hoax someone', 'pull his leg'.

boniment (m). 'Hot air' or 'propaganda', a lot of jabber signifying
nothing or including a good deal of exaggeration. *Bonimenter*
is the verb (*v.* also ARTICLE). *Faire du boniment* can mean
'to give a lot of sales talk'. *Fariboles* (q.v.) is somewhat similar. *Il dit des fariboles*, 'He talks nonsense'.

bonneterie (f). On the off chance that you want to buy a bonnet,
be forewarned: you find almost everything (for women) but
bonnets in a *bonneterie*. You find stockings (*des bas*), first of
all; the extension to *gaines* and *jupons* ('girdles' and 'petti-
coats') and *lingerie* in general is easy, and may go so far as
maillots de bain, pantalons, corsages, 'pulls' ('swimsuits', 'slacks',
'blouses', 'sweaters') and—as near as you'll get to a bonnet—
foulards.
In motoring terms, 'the bonnet' (US: 'hood') is *le capot*.
(*v.* the chapter on LA VOITURE.)

boom (m). Used in financial circles to mean a 'boom'; while in
students circles *une boum* means 'a dance', 'a soiree', 'a gala'.
Une surboum is along the same lines, while *une surprise party
[sic]* is a smaller, more intimate evening's dancing and drinking, usually at someone's house.

bouger. You know that this means 'to move', 'to budge'. But when you buy a tablecloth, for instance, you are wise to ask *Est-ce qu'elle bougera au lavage?* 'Will it shrink in the wash?' A more colloquial term than *rétrécir*.

Avoir la bougeotte is a different matter: 'to be restless'. Rather *familier*.

bougie (f). The ordinary candle, more ordinary (*grossière*) than *une chandelle*, which is longer and thinner. Neither word suits the taper used in the church, which is *un cierge*.

When the garage mechanic tells you that you have *une bougie qui est morte*, he is referring to a spark(ing-)plug! (*v.* the chapter on LA VOITURE.)

Une vente à la bougie is, like *une vente aux enchères*, 'an auction sale'. The 'Going—Going—Gone' is expressed by the successive extinguishing of three candles placed in front of the auctioneer, *le commissaire-priseur*.

bougnat (m). Neighborhood retailer of coal, butane gas, and wood. Usually a den of a shop with *un comptoir* which makes it something of a *bistro* (or *bistrot*) as well, and you will see *café-bois-charbons* written over the door. Legend has it that every other *Auvergnat* who comes to settle in Paris becomes *un bougnat*.

bouquet (m). 'A bouquet', or 'clump' of trees as well as flowers. Also familiar to wine lovers, as the 'aroma of wine'.

C'est le bouquet! 'That's the end!' 'That's torn it!' See also, in the same vein, COMBLE, COMMODE, COMPLET.

bourratif. Definitely colloquial, and meaning 'filling', as applied to a dish or course. *Les spaghetti sont très bourratifs.* 'Spaghetti is very filling.'

By the way, when at table your hostess urges you to take another helping, don't try to build an analogy on *bourratif* and say, *merci, je suis bourré(e)*. But above all, you must never say *je suis plein(e)*, since *être pleine* applies only to animals and means 'to be big with young'. There are several polite unaffected ways of saying 'no, thank you'. *Merci, c'est délicieux mais je n'ai plus faim*; or *merci, je me suis déjà bien servi*; or simply *non merci*. You may also run across *je ne peux plus*, but this is reserved for occasions when you know your *convives*, your 'fellow guests', really very well.

bout (m). One of those little words which lends itself to a dozen expressions, many of which find ample explanation in any good dictionary. Let us recall particularly: *je suis à bout*, 'I've had it.' 'I can't take any more.'

Ça fait un petit bout d'ici. 'It's a fair distance from here.' *Nous avons fait un petit bout de chemin ensemble.* 'We travelled a little way together.'

If you want to say 'at the end of the room', *à la fin* will never do; you need *au bout de la pièce*, or *dans le fond*.

Un bout of something is 'a bit', 'a scrap'. *Il n'a pas pu nous proposer mieux qu'un petit bout du gigot de la veille.* 'He had nothing more to offer than a scrap of yesterday's leg of lamb'. *Elle a mangé du bout des lèvres.* 'She just nibbled.'

But *un petit bout de chou* belongs in a non-culinary context; this corresponds to 'little lamb', 'sweetie pie', in other words, 'a baby'.

A bout de bras, 'at arm's length'.

Joindre les deux bouts, 'to make both ends meet'.

boutique (f). 'Shop'; as distinct from *un magasin*, which is bigger, and *un grand magasin*, which is a 'department store'. *Parler boutique*, 'to talk shop'. The shopkeeper is *le boutiquier*.

box (m). Not 'a box' (*v.* BOÎTE), but that much-sought-after convenience, especially in Paris, 'a garage', 'a private and covered parking place', often bought or rented with one's flat. The plural is *boxes*.

La boxe, despite its gender, is the masculine sport of boxing; 'a boxer' is *un boxeur*.

brancher. 'To plug in' a lamp or other electrical appliance. *Débrancher* is 'to unplug'. *La prise* and *le fil* are, respectively, 'the plug' and 'the wire.' 'A fuse' is *un plomb*, q.v. (*v.* also AMPOULE).

A branch of a large store is not *'branche'*—that would be too easy—but *une succursale*, and you will sometimes see it abbreviated on awnings and so on as *Succ.*

bribes (f. pl.). Always used in the plural. Something of a false friend, perhaps, since it means 'scraps', 'odd leftovers' (of food, cloth, even conversation overheard), and has nothing to do with the English word 'bribe',which is *un pot-de-vin*.

bricole (f). Any thing or affair of minimal importance. *Bricoler* means 'to putter *or* mess about', 'to do it yourself', 'make something' or 'put something together'. *Un bricoleur* is the person addicted to doing it himself, *le bricolage.*

brin (m). A word that lends itself to many figurative uses. You have not only *un brin d'herbe*, 'a blade of grass'; but *un brin de conversation* (or *de causette*), 'a chat'; and *un brin de bon sens*, usually used in the negative: *elle n'a pas un brin de bon sens*, 'she hasn't a scrap of common sense'. *Un beau brin de fille*, 'a fine strapping girl'.

brosser. 'To brush', of course. But *brosser un tableau* has the strictly figurative idea of sketching the general outline of a situation. *Notre conférencier d'aujourd'hui va vous brosser un tableau de la situation au Viet-nam.* 'Today's lecturer will outline for you the state of affairs in Vietnam' (*v.* also DRESSER).

bureau (m). 'A desk'. Also, 'an office'; except that of a *notaire(une étude)*, and that of a doctor, dentist, or barrister (US: lawyer), *un cabinet.* Among the more common office items are:

agrafe (f): 'staple'.
agrafeuse (f): 'stapler'.
bic (m): 'ball-point pen'.
bloc (m): 'tablet *or* pad of paper'.
buvard (m): 'blotter'.
  papier buvard (m): 'blotting paper'.
cahier (m): 'notebook'.
chemise (f): 'Manila folder'.
classer : 'to file'.
classeur (m): 'filing cabinet'.
clavier (m): 'keyboard' (of typewriter).
comptabilité (f): 'accounting department'.
  comptable (m): 'accountant'.
corbeille à papiers (f): 'wastepaper basket'.
coupe-papier (m): 'letter opener', 'paper cutter'.
courrier (m): 'post', 'mail'.
craie (f): 'chalk'.
crayon (m): 'pencil'.
dictaphone (m): 'dictaphone'.
  dicter: 'to dictate'.
dossier (m): 'file' (documents).
double (m): 'carbon copy'.
élastique (m): 'rubber band'.
encre (f): 'ink'.
enveloppe (f): 'envelope'.
facture (f): 'bili', 'invoice'.
fiche (f): 'index card'.
fichier (m): 'card index'.
gomme (f): 'eraser'.
machine à écrire (f): 'typewriter'.
  taper: 'to type'.
photocopie (f): 'photocopy'.
punaise (f): 'drawing-pin' (US: 'thumbtack').
registre (m): 'register', 'record book'.
règle (f): 'ruler'.
Scotch (m) or *papier collant* (m): 'Scotch tape'(trade name).
standard (m): 'telephone switchboard'.
  standardiste (f): 'operator'.
stylo (m): 'fountain pen'.
  stylo à bille (m): 'ball-point pen'; *v.* BIC.
tampon (m): 'rubber stamp'.
timbre (m): 'postage stamp'.
touche (f): 'key' (of typewriter).
trombone (m): 'paper clip'.

(*v.* also DACTYLO; PAPIER; VIRGULE; and the chapter on LE TÉLÉPHONE.)

C

ça. The contraction of *cela*, as you know. But you must also remember that *ça* is far more 'spoken,' so that when you are writing, especially a formal report or dissertation, or even a letter to someone you don't know well, *cela* is definitely called for.

cabinets (m. pl.). A polite word for 'the lavatory'. *Où sont les cabinets?* (*v.* also LAVABO).

In the singular, *cabinet* does mean, among other things, a 'ministerial Cabinet'. *Un conseil de cabinet,* 'a Cabinet meeting'. And *le cabinet* is the word for a 'law office' or 'doctor's office' (*v.* BUREAU).

cachet (m). The equivalent of 'tablet' in terms of aspirin and so on, and it is on an equal footing with *un comprimé. Une pilule,* however, is supposedly rounder than either of the above.

Since *un cachet* is also 'seal' or 'imprint', *le cachet de la poste* is the 'postmark' on a letter. The rules of a contest may stipulate that *le cachet de la poste fera foi*: 'compliance with the deadline, *or* the earlier of two entries, will be determined by the postmark'.

Or again, this is a word you want to remember when called upon to pay a compliment to something even if it is not really attractive: *Ah oui, ce fauteuil a un certain cachet, indiscutablement.* 'Oh dear, yes, that armchair certainly is distinctive (chic, charming, etc.).' You can apply this to smaller objects, or to a style or a manner, to mean the distinction or a charm peculiar to the thing in question.

cadre (m). What *l'encadreur* will put around your paintings, mirrors, and so on. But *un cadre* is not only 'a frame'; it is also a person who forms part of the higher or administrative personnel of a firm. *Son filleul monte vite: il fait maintenant partie des cadres.* 'His godson is going places fast; he's on the managerial staff now.' *La formation des cadres* means 'the training of employees (*or* of students in special schools) for executive posts'.

cake (m). A special sort of *Faux Ami*, bred by Franglais: 'fruit-cake' only. Any other sort of cake is *un gâteau* or *une pâtisserie. Cake* is pronounced as in English.

calé. Without going into the verb as a whole, we would like to stress an extremely common use made of its past participle as an adjective to indicate that someone is '*très fort*,' 'very well qualified' or 'well up on something'. *Elle est très calée en mathématiques.* 'She's very strong in math.' *Il a entrepris des études calées.* 'He has undertaken difficult studies.'

camper. 'To camp out'; also called *faire du camping* (*v.* the chapter on FRANGLAIS). *Camper un personnage* is a very handy phrase for the student called upon to criticize a work of literature and is fondly used by book reviewers. It means 'to make a given character three-dimensional, believable'.

capitaine d'industrie (m). 'A big businessman', an important *homme d'affaires*; and not to be confused with *un chevalier d'industrie*, 'a shady businessman', 'shark', or 'confidence man'.

car (m). A troublesome *Faux Ami*. Not 'a car' at all, which is *une voiture*, but 'an interurban *or* touring coach' (US: 'bus'). 'A city bus' is *un (auto)bus*.

caractère (m). Very frequently used to describe someone's temperament or nature. *La tradition veut que toute belle-mère ait mauvais caractère.* 'Tradition has it that all mothers-in-law are sour-tempered, *or* mean.' *Il a beau avoir bon caractère, il y a une limite à tout.* 'Good-natured as he is, there is a limit.' *Elle a un caractère assez égal.* 'She is even-tempered.' You will often find *être de bonne (mauvaise) composition* instead of *avoir bon (mauvais) caractère*.
   Avoir du caractère, or *faire preuve de caractère*, 'to have character'.
   'A character' ('He's a real character!') is *un original*; 'a fictional character' is *un personnage*.

caravane (f). Coming into use more and more, at the expense of *roulotte* (f), to mean 'a caravan' (US: 'trailer'), or house on wheels pulled by a car. *La roulotte* by now means a 'gipsy caravan' first of all, if not exclusively.

carie (f). 'A cavity', in the dental sense. 'The filling' is *un plombage*. If you're unlucky it may become necessary to *arracher la dent*, a vigorous way of saying 'to pull the tooth'. While the operation goes on, you will be seated in *le fauteuil du dentiste*, since 'the dentist's chair' is an armchair in French (and in fact).

carré. An adjective that has nothing to do with the recent expression 'square', meaning 'not with the trend', or as the younger French generation would have it, *'pas dans le vent'*. No, it means 'straightforward', 'frank', 'blunt'. *Carrément* is 'frankly', 'without beating about the bush'. *Mais demande-lui donc carrément une augmentation.* 'But just ask him straight out for a raise.' *Il est carré en affaires.* 'He is plain-dealing, straightforward in business.'

cartouche (f). Not only any sort of 'cartridge' (as in your fountain pen, for instance), but 'a carton of cigarettes'. You should be warned, however, that cigarettes are not generally sold by the carton in France.

cas (m). Again, the basis of a multitude of expressions. One which may not appear in the dictionary is *un cas* when speaking of someone: 'He's a real case, really singular *or* special.' *Ah celui-là, c'est un cas.*

And *un en cas* is 'a snack', 'a stopgap', or 'pack lunch', *en cas* (or *dans le cas*) *où vous en auriez besoin.*

casserole (f). 'A cooking pot *or* pan', and not what it has come to mean by extension in English: 'a one-dish meal', which would be *un plat.*

catch (m). A fine old Franglais word, meaning 'wrestling'. *Un catcheur* is, logically, 'a wrestler'.

'The catch' or 'clasp' of a necklace, coffer, and so on is *un fermoir.*

ça va (*allait, ira, irait*). An indispensable but dangerous catch-all, as it is tempting to make use of it ten times more often than one should, at the expense of more precise vocabulary. When you greet someone whom you've already met and know rather well, you say *Comment ça va?* or simply *Ça va?*, and the someone replies *Ça va et vous?* (*et toi?*), or *Ça va comme ci-comme ça*, or *Ça ne va pas très fort*, etc. *Ça va?*, then, can mean 'How are you?' 'How are things?' 'Is it all right?' and the answer, *Ça va* (*bien*), means 'OK, fine, everything's all right'. *Je me sens fatigué mais ça ira mieux demain.* 'I feel tired, but I'll be all right tomorrow.'

Again, *ça va* may often be used in pairs: *Bon bon, ça va ça va.* 'All right, all right, that's enough'; or 'OK, I've got the idea.'

ça y est (*était, sera, serait*). Another jack-of-all-trades sort of expression; heard again and again, in any context, and often used to announce an action beginning or completed, quite like 'there!', 'got it!', 'I did it', 'there they go', 'that's that'. *Ils craignaient que leur fils ne réussisse pas son bachot, mais ça y est.* 'They were afraid their son would not pull off his exam, but he got through it all right.' *Venez voir le feu d'artifice—ça y est, ils ont commencé.* 'Come quick and see the fireworks—there, now they've started.'

As a question, *ça y est?* can just as easily take on any shade of meaning: 'Have you got it?' 'Is it over?'

You can easily see the rather vague, often unsatisfying quality of this expression, and why you should be careful of overdoing it.

cellule (f). 'A cell', in any sense—blood, prison, monastery. But you may need to take special note of other meanings: 'the light meter' of your camera, and 'a communist cell'.

ce que. There is surely no need to remind you of all the grammar which attaches to *ce que.* But one colloquial use of *ce que* which often does not appear in the grammar book is the exclamatory: *Ce qu'il peut être bête!* 'Incredible how stupid he can be!' *Ce que ce film m'a plu!* 'Oh, I loved that film!' *Ce* *qu'ils ont dû s'ennuyer!* 'How bored they must have been!' As you will have realized already, *ce que* used in this way is simply an abridged form of *Qu'est-ce que*, or a substitute for *comme . . . Comme il est grand! Ce qu'il est grand!*

c'est-à-dire. 'That is to say'; and as you would expect, it is used (and abused) as often as are 'that is', or 'I mean' in English. Or again, it's a ready-made question formula, just like 'meaning?' or 'that is?', but in this capacity it is likely to sound as ill-bred or abrupt as its English counterparts.

chagrin (m). This may well mean general 'sadness' or 'tearfulness' and apply as well to a child who bursts into tears as to an adult: *Le pauvre petit, il a un gros chagrin.* The verb, *chagriner* or *être chagriné*, is not so commonly used.

chahuter. Roughly, 'to heckle', or 'deliberately to interrupt' (a speaker) with boisterous or disorderly behavior. *Dans la classe de sciences naturelles, on ne chahute jamais.* 'In the natural sciences class (or classroom; *v.* CLASSE), there is never any problem of discipline.' *Le candidat a été pas mal chahuté pendant son discours.* 'The candidate was the object of quite a lot of heckling during his speech.'

chambre (f). 'A room'; almost exclusively 'a bedroom' although more properly speaking, the full name is *une chambre à coucher.*
   Une chambrée is 'a military barracks'; *un dortoir*, 'dormitory' (i.e. a large room with many beds).
   Chambrer is 'to warm (red) wine'—theoretically 'to room temperature', *à la température ambiante.*

chameau (m). When someone is disagreeable, quarrelsome, mean, you call him or her *vieux chameau, va!*—literally, 'nasty old camel'—and immediately you feel better. This is standard form for speaking disrespectfully of a mother-in-law: *mon chameau de belle-mère.* Or you may find *la vache!* as soothing as *chameau!* (*v.* the chapter on LANGAGE FAMILIER).
   There are of course a number of expressions using animals. You might note that *un âne* is 'a dunce', 'an imbecile'; and *une ânerie*, 'a stupid thing to do'. *Avoir un chat dans la gorge* translates 'to have a frog in your throat', and *avoir la puce à l'oreille* is 'to smell a rat.'

champignon (m). The noble 'mushroom'. Beware, when you buy mushrooms in the market, of the way in which the price is indicated: not per *kilogramme* (2·2 pounds), as with most fruit and vegetables, but by 250 *gr.* or *la demi-livre*, and occasionally even by 100 *gr.*
   Le champignon is also, colloquially, 'the accelerator' in the car; *écraser le champignon*, 'to step hard on the accelerator' (US: 'the gas').

chance (f). A classic *Faux Ami*, as it does not mean 'chance', but 'luck'. If you say *j'ai eu la chance de le rencontrer*, you are saying 'I was lucky enough to meet him'; whereas perhaps you meant 'I had a chance to meet him': *j'ai eu l'occasion de le rencontrer* (*v.* OCCASION).

Pas de chance! 'Bad luck!' *La malchance*, 'bad luck'.
Bonne chance! 'Good luck!'

chandelle (f). 'A candle', generally slenderer and more elegant than *une bougie* (q.v.). Where you might use the latter in an emergency, when the fuses blow (*v.* PLOMB), a *chandelle* is what you want when you dress up the dinner table for a *dîner aux chandelles*.

Devoir une fière chandelle à quelqu'un means 'to have real cause to be grateful'. *Il vous doit une fière chandelle.* 'He owes you an awful lot.'

En voir trente-six chandelles, 'to be knocked unconscious'. *En tombant elle a dû se cogner contre la poignée, elle en a vu trente-six chandelles.* 'She must have struck the doorhandle as she fell; she was knocked out.'

chanter. A verb that is straightforward enough, you say: it means 'to sing'. And so it does; but in certain *milieux* or circumstances it can mean 'to talk', 'to open up', 'give away secrets'. *Faire chanter* is 'to blackmail'; *le chantage* is 'blackmail' itself; and the person responsible, 'the blackmailer', is *le maître chanteur*—a term which has no feminine form. . . . When *quelque chose chante à quelqu'un*, then 'something appeals to, *or* tempts, someone'. *Aller au concert cet après-midi? oui, ça me chante.* 'Yes, I feel like going to a concert this afternoon.' This is distinctly a colloquial use of the verb, and you will want to be careful not to overuse or to write it.

chapeau (m). 'A hat', as you know. But if ever you've had any experience of student restaurants in France, you will remember the swelling cry of 'chapeau!' that went up from the assembled eaters each time some innocent appeared in the cafeteria line with a hat on, this being curiously taboo in student circles. The cry is repeated mercilessly until the guilty person, blushing, removes the offending article. But *chapeau!* or *chapeau bas!* can also express congratulations or admiration, more informally than *félicitations!* 'Hats off!'

La chapellerie is the art or trade of hat-making; while *un chapelier* sells men's hats, *la modiste* sells women's or children's.

La chapelure is something else altogether: 'breadcrumbs', such as those used in making 'breaded veal cutlets' (*côtes de veau panées*).

chargé. Literally, 'loaded'. In current use, it means therefore 'busy', 'occupied', 'full'. *Que personne ne me dérange, j'ai une matinée très chargée.* 'I don't want anyone to bother me; I've got a very busy morning ahead of me.' *Messieurs, nous abordons* *ce matin le programme de la semaine: il est très chargé.* 'This morning, gentlemen, we shall take up the week's program, which is a very heavy one.'

If you want to translate 'he is loaded (with money)', then you say *il est bourré de fric* (*v.* the chapter on LANGAGE FAMILIER).

chemise (f.). 'A man's shirt', although the word is feminine; whereas a woman's blouse, particularly of the button-down-the-front variety, is a masculine word, *un chemisier.* (*Le ch misier* is also 'the shirtmaker'.) A blouse of a less mantailored sort is likely to be *un corsage.* A nightgown is *une chemise de nuit,* and may be accompanied by *un peignoir, un déshabillé,* or *une robe de chambre.* (The latter term applies as well to a man's as to a woman's bathrobe or dressing gown.) *Etre en bras de chemise,* or *en manches de chemise,* 'to be in shirtsleeves'.

Une chemise can also be 'a (manila) folder', for filing or protecting papers. (*v.* BUREAU.)

If it's 'an undershirt' you want, then you mean *un maillot de corps.*

And you need to be careful about *une blouse* (pronounced 'blues'), which nowadays has rarely anything to do with a woman's blouse. It means 'a smock', for artist, housewife, or nursery-school child (and may then also be called *un tablier*), or a doctor's or nurse's white coat. You are right, of course, in protesting that *un tablier* is also 'an apron', of the kitchen or hostess variety.

chercher. *Chercher* has more than its grammar book meaning of 'to look for', 'to seek'. It can be used for: 'to pick up' or 'to collect', in quite the same way as *prendre. Ils viendront demain chercher le tapis pour le nettoyer.* 'The cleaners are coming to pick up the rug tomorrow.' *Il faut que j'aille à l'autre bout de Paris chercher ma voiture neuve.* 'I have to go all the way over to the other side of Paris to pick up my new car.'

Il ne faut pas chercher à comprendre is one of those marvellous *phrases toutes faites.* Literally, 'you must not seek to understand', which is decidedly too oracular: 'there's no explanation, no rhyme or reason'; or 'it's beyond me', or 'just accept (the situation) as it is'.

Vous l'avez cherché is like *c'est bien fait pour vous*: 'you asked for it', 'it's your own fault', 'it serves you right'. Not a very endearing thing to say, any more than 'I told you so' is.

And again, there is the *chercher* which can mean 'cost up to'. *Si vous voulez une bonne reproduction de ce tableau, attention, cela peut aller chercher jusque dans les 3,000 francs.* 'If you want a good reproduction of this painting, be forewarned; it can go as high as 3,000 francs.'

cheveux (m. pl.). 'Hair', in general. *Il s'est fait couper les cheveux en brosse.* 'He's had a crewcut.' *La chevelure* is 'the head of hair'. *Ce qui fait la beauté de cette fille, c'est sa chevelure* *abondante.* 'The stunning thing about that girl is her thick hair.' *Un cheveu* is 'a (strand of) hair', while *un poil* is 'an isolated hair *or* bristle'; *les poils d'une moustache ou d'une barbe, les poils de sanglier d'une brosse, les poils d'une fourrure ou d'une bête.* But: *Il perd ses cheveux,* 'he's going bald'. Baldness is *la calvitie;* the adjective is *chauve.* Your 'scalp' is *le cuir chevelu.* And when the wind blows your hair about, you are *échevelé,* 'dishevelled'. *Poilu,* as an adjective, is 'hirsute', 'hairy'. As a nickname, it refers to the French infantryman in World War I.

Poil figures in a couple of colloquial expressions. *Avoir un poil dans la main,* 'to be extremely lazy'. *Il n'a plus un poil d'accent en français.* 'He hasn't the least trace of accent any more in French.'

Another very informal phrase is *arriver comme les cheveux sur la soupe:* 'to be very much out of place, unexpected, incongruous'.

Une explication tirée par les cheveux is 'a far-fetched explanation'. And surely there is no need to remind you that *couper les cheveux en quatre* is simply 'to split hairs'.

chiffon (m). The humble 'duster', or any scrap of cloth. *J'aurai juste le temps de donner un coup de chiffon.* 'I'll have just enough time to do some quick dusting.' *Chiffonner,* however, does not mean 'to dust' (*épousseter*), but 'to crumple' or 'wrinkle'; and also, figuratively, 'to vex' or 'annoy'. *Cette nouvelle le chiffonne.* 'This piece of news troubles him.' *Un minois chiffonné* is either 'a weary face' or a young woman's face with irregular but pleasant features.

circulation (f). A word you can hear all too often, since everyone agrees that there is too much of it: 'road traffic'. *Circuler,* or *rouler, en voiture* means 'to go by car'. *L'agent de police,* exasperated, will shout: *Mais circulez plus vite, Monsieur, circulez plus vite!* Of course you may also apply circulation to blood: *la circulation sanguine.*

And although *trafiquer* and *un trafiquant* do exist, they are *Faux Amis,* since they have to do with 'trade' and 'dealings', usually illegal: *le trafic de la drogue,* 'narcotics trade'. Yet *le trafic routier* is a term which you may safely use for 'traffic on main roads'.

cireur (m). 'Bootblack' or 'shoe-shine boy'. At the entry of most Métro stations in Paris, you will see *WC—Cireurs,* meaning that these conveniences are to be found underground, inside the station.

Cirer is 'to wax' or 'polish' (parquet flooring, furniture, shoes). *La cire* is 'wax', such as candles are made of, whereas *le cirage* is shoe (or other) polish. *Etre dans le cirage,* 'to be in a fog'.

ciseau (m). 'A chisel.' If it's 'scissors' you want, then you must say *les ciseaux* or *une paire de ciseaux.*

claque (f). There are nine chances in ten that if you cross *un square* where children are playing in *le tas de sable*, the sand-pile, you will hear *une maman* say to *son petit*: '*Veux-tu une paire de claques?*' 'If you don't behave I'll slap you.' *Une gifle* is a less colloquial term for 'slap'.

If the play you've gone to see is *un four,* 'a flop', the only people likely to be applauding are *la claque*, those planted in the audience with the express purpose of clapping. *Rentrer claqué de son travail* is 'to come home exhausted from work'. A bit *familier.   Prière de ne pas claquer la porte en sortant* is an injunction not to slam the door on your way out.

classe (f). In scholastic terms, either 'the class', i.e. 'the course', or 'the classroom' itself. In office terminology, *classer* means 'to file', in *un classeur* (*v.* BUREAU).

In general, *classe* and *classer* can be used as you would 'class' or 'rank' in English. 'The working class' in not *la classe travaillante* or any other participial term but *la classe ouvrière*. Yet the participle holds good for the 'governing *or* ruling class': *la classe dirigeante*. In military terms, *faire ses classes* is 'to go through training camp'.

clou (m). 'A nail', of the sort you drive into a wall. A fingernail is *un ongle*; a toenail, *un ongle de doigt de pied*.

The *clou de la soirée* or *du spectacle* is 'the star attraction', the act which steals the limelight.

Mettre quelque chose au clou is 'to pawn it', to leave it with *un prêteur sur gages* (*v.* MONT-DE-PIÉTÉ).

coffre-fort (m). 'A strongbox' or 'safe',   or a safe-deposit box at the bank (*v.* the chapter on LA BANQUE).

coincer. 'To catch', 'trap', 'wedge', 'put in a tight corner'. Very commonly heard, in both literal and figurative use. *L'ascenseur est coincé entre deux étages.* 'The lift is stuck between two floors.' *J'ai deux rendez-vous pour 10h, me voilà coincé!* 'I've got two 10 o'clock appointments. I'm stuck!'

combinaison (f). A dictionary will tell you that this is 'a pair of overalls', such as a garage mechanic wears. But women especially need to know that this is 'a slip', the feminine undergarment. The word *slip* (m) does exist—but means 'underpants', the more exact term for which, for a woman, would be *une culotte* anyhow. 'A half-slip' or 'petticoat' is *un jupon.*

Combinaison also means 'a scheme' or 'plot'; a more *familier* (and sometimes pejorative) term is *la combine*, which is at the basis of *le Système D* (*v.* DÉBROUILLER).

comble (m). Included here to remind you of *c'est le comble!* and similar   ironic expressions with *bouquet, complet, commode* (q.v.): 'That's just fine!'

comédien (m). A reminder that *un(e) comédien(ne)* means 'an actor' ('actress') and does not by any means necessarily imply a comic actor, or what English calls 'a comedian'. The primary meaning of *La Comédie Française* is simply 'The French Theatre'. On the other hand, *jouer la comédie* does mean 'to put on an act', 'to play-act', or even 'to act up'. *Avec son grand-père, qui est très sévère, elle ne joue jamais la comédie.* 'When with her grandfather, who is quite strict, she never puts on an act.' You may call 'a comedy' either *une comédie* or *une pièce comique* and 'a tragedy' either *une tragédie* or *une pièce tragique*.

Le dramaturge is the 'dramatist' or 'playwright'.

comment. Another of those omnipresent and all-purpose words. First of all, as a question, meaning *Je n'ai pas compris*, but less polite by far than *Je vous demande pardon?* or *Je m'excuse?* 'I beg your pardon?'

And then of course, meaning 'how?' *Comment a-t-il fait son compte pour arriver si tard?* 'How did he manage to get there so late?' *Et comment!* 'And how!'

Beware of the all-too-lazy *comment dirai-je?* or simply, *comment dire?* or *comment dit-on?* 'how shall I say?' 'what do you call it?' *Lors de la représentation, j'ai ressenti, comment dirai-je, un sentiment, comment dire, d'angoisse, enfin, comment dit-on, d'inquiétude,* 'During the performance I felt, what shall I say, a feeling of, well, anxiety, I mean uneasiness, what do you call it?'

Comment!, in a vehemently exclamatory tone, can mean 'well, of all the nerve!' or 'what on earth!' or any other vigorous expression of indignation. *Comment! tu t'es permis de l'inviter sans me prévenir!* 'Well, of all the . . . You took it on yourself to invite him without informing me!' *Ça alors!* expresses the same feeling, more familiarly.

The English verb 'to comment' is *commenter*, or *faire un commentaire* or *une remarque*.

commode. Certainly one of the more common adjectives, meaning 'handy', 'convenient', 'readily feasible'. *Cet instrument est très commode pour dénoyauter les olives.* 'That's a very handy gadget for stoning (US: pitting) olives.'

Ce n'est pas commode pour aller chez lui. 'It's not very easy to get to his place.' *Elle n'est pas commode.* 'She's not easy to get along with.'

Often used with irony, to mean just the opposite of convenient: *Alors ça par exemple! C'est commode!* 'Well now that's just fine (the end, all I needed, too much).' In this connection, v. also BOUQUET, COMBLE, COMPLET.

complet. You may apply this to any public conveyance or hall which is full; the bus conductor will pull down the little *COMPLET* sign at the back of the bus (usually, some time after the bus has become full, but never mind). At a concert hall, this is the equivalent of 'Sold Out' or 'Standing room only'—except that French theatres and auditoriums rarely if ever sell standing room.

Un complet or *un complet veston* is commonly called *un costume*: 'a man's suit.' Also: *C'est complet!* 'It's the last straw.' (*v.* also BOUQUET, COMMODE, COMBLE.)

compteur (m). 'The meter': *compteur à gaz, compteur électrique.* When you rent a flat or a room, you do well to ask whether *le gaz et l'électricité* (and even *l'eau*) *sont compris dans le prix,* included in the price, or whether they are *en plus,* in which case they will often be calculated *sur la base du compteur individuel* in your lodgings.

concours (m). 'A competition' or 'a competitive examination'. *Il a été reçu premier au concours d'entrée à Scienccs Po.* 'He got the top score on the competitive entry exam for (the *Ecole des) Sciences Politiques.' Pour être Agrégé, il faut réussir le concours de l'Agrégation, alors que le Doctorat est une question de thèse.* 'To receive the title of *Agrégé,* you have to pass the competitive exam called the *Agrégation,* whereas to get your doctorate, you write a thesis.'

Le concours also signifies *l'aide, l'assistance. Notre émission a été réalisée avec le concours d'Untel*: 'Our program was produced with the collaboration of So-and-So'. *Prêter son concours à une vente de charité* might be translated 'to help organize a charity bazaar'.

conditionnel (m). A verb in the conditional tense may require a second reading, since this tense is often used with the force of *'paraît-il'*: 'it would seem that', 'he is said to have . . .' *Les forces du sud auraient détruit trois ponts.* 'The southern army is said to have knocked out three bridges.' *Il ne serait pas rentré chez lui depuis dimanche.* 'Apparently he hasn't been home since Sunday.'

A special instance of this special use of the conditional is the verb *savoir:* it may take on the meaning of *pouvoir. On ne saurait trop vous conseiller cette solution.* 'We cannot recommend that solution too highly.'

conduire. 'To drive (a car)', 'to lead', 'guide', 'direct'. *A gauche du salon est un long couloir conduisant vers les chambres.* 'To the left of the living room is a long corridor leading to the bedrooms.' *Attendez l'ouvreuse, elle vous conduira à vos places.* 'Wait for the usherette, who will show you to your seats.'

But look again at some of the pitfalls awaiting the speaker whose native tongue is English: *Un conducteur* is 'a driver' (of a car), but this is not the word you want for 'an orchestra conductor', who is *un chef d'orchestre.* His function is *diriger l'orchestre.* If you are talking about a musical group other than an orchestra—*un ensemble vocal ou instrumental*—then you had better say that it is *dirigé par Untel,* or that it is *placé sous la direction d'Untel.*

Similarly, the conductor of a train, bus, or tram cannot be called *le conducteur* but *le receveur*. 'The driver's license' is *le permis de conduire* (*v*. the chapter on LA VOITURE.)

confection (f). Nothing to do with confectionery or sweets; for this you need *la confiserie*, which is at once the shop selling sweets, the making of them, and the sweet itself.

La confection is the making of clothes and hence 'ready-made clothes' themselves, also called *le prêt-à-porter*, as distinct from *les vêtements sur mesure*, 'clothing made to measure'. But *c'est elle qui a fait sa robe de mariée*. 'She made her own wedding gown.'

congé (m). The meaning of *congé* that most people are interested in is that of holidays; *les congés payés* is the minimum annual holiday period, from three to four weeks, that the law requires every employer to pay his workers. *Un congé de maladie* is 'sick leave'; *un congé de maternité* 'pregnancy leave'. 'A military leave' is generally *une permission*.

A couple of expressions which may be troublesome because of their resemblance are: *prendre congé de quelqu'un*, and *donner congé à quelqu'un*. The first, like *quitter*, means 'to take leave of someone', while the second, like *congédier*, is 'to dismiss (sack) someone'.

congélateur (m). 'The freezing compartment' of a refrigerator, or 'a freezer' by itself; also often called *un freezer . . . Un réfrigérateur* may also be styled *un frigidaire*.

conserver. 'To preserve'. *Elle est bien conservée pour son âge.* 'She appears young (is well preserved) for her age.' *Les conserves* are 'tinned (US: canned) goods'; *en conserve* means 'preserved', when speaking of food.

Le conservateur d'un musée is 'the curator of a museum'; he may also be *conservateur* (adj.) in the political sense: 'conservative'. If he is a she, she is *Madame la conservatrice* (sometimes even *Madame le conservateur*) and she may be *conservatrice* (adj.) in her opinions.

consigne (f). Your first encounter with *la consigne* will undoubtedly occur at *la gare*: you will look for the 'cloak- *or* checkroom', and this is it. And next, if you go to pick up a bottle of something at the wine merchant's or the grocer's (*le marchand de vins* or *l'épicier*), you may well pay a *consigne*, a 'deposit' on the bottle, or on a jar of jam. If not, the bottle (or jar) may be marked *verre* (or *pot*) *perdu*, since there is no return on your payment.

If you are called upon to *prendre les consignes* of a particular job, you are to take over from the post's present occupant and go through a prior period of instruction or familiarization.

And if you are a pupil (*un élève*), you will quickly come to know that *être consigné* means 'to be told to stay after school' or 'to come to school on the Thursday or the Saturday afternoon'; at any rate, 'to be punished' (*v*. PROFESSEUR).

consommation (f). The drink you order in a café.

constater. A verb you hear very frequently; it has something of a scientific ring to it, as it means 'to notice', 'remark', 'observe'. *Mais, cher monsieur, je ne vous accuse point, je constate, voilà tout.* 'But, my good man, I'm not accusing you; I'm merely stating.' *On a pu constater une diminution du nombre de spectateurs dans les cinémas.* 'A drop in attendance at the cinema (US: movies) has been observed.' The noun is *la constatation.*

à contre-cœur. How often do English-speaking people struggle to find the word for 'reluctantly' in French, and attempt to make do with *'contre la volonté'* or some such analogy to 'unwillingly'. The trouble is that the Frenchman in this case is not acting against his will but against his heart: *à contre-cœur*; or again, *le cœur n'y est (était, etc.) pas.*

corde (f). The meanings of this word are pretty straightforward, and amply set forth in any dictionary: 'twine', and so on. But 'a musical chord' is *un accord*, and if you want to talk about 'electric cord *or* wire', you need the word *fil (électrique)* (m). And if *quelque chose n'est pas dans les cordes de quelqu'un* the person is not very well qualified to do something. *Les maths ne sont pas dans ses cordes.* 'Mathematics are not really his line, his strong point.'

correct. Something of a *Faux Ami*; for although it can mean 'correct' in the sense of 'exact' or 'accurate' or 'right', it equates more often with 'polite', 'decent', 'well-bred', 'proper'. *Ils l'ont licencié le mois dernier, mais ils ont été corrects (l'ont fait correctement).* 'They gave him the sack last month, but they were decent about it.' *Elle est d'une correction exemplaire.* 'Her conduct (*or* breeding) is irreproachable.' *Ce film était presque incorrect.* 'That film was practically indecent.' 'To correct' may be expressed by *corriger* or *reprendre.*

couleurs, marchand de (m). He is sometimes hard to distinguish from *le quincaillier* and, to complicate things further, *le marchand de couleurs* may, or used to, be called *le droguiste* and his shop, *la droguerie.* Let's make a very rough distinction: *la boutique du marchand de couleurs* is more of a woman's haven, with anything from *toile cirée* ('oilcloth'), paints, soap, frying pans and toilet paper to disposable nappies (US: diapers), all plastic and metal gadgets for the home, shampoos, and Christmas tree ornaments. But *la quincaillerie* has an unmistakably masculine atmosphere, being a businesslike storehouse limited strictly to tools, screws, nuts, bolts and nails, and catering not only to the Sunday *bricoleur* but also to the professional carpenter, mason, and others.

En faire voir à quelqu'un de toutes les couleurs is a quite *familier* expression, meaning 'to give someone a very bad time of it', 'put someone through an awful lot' (*v.* also BLEU).

coup (m). Certainly one of the master keys to any number of linguistic doors which otherwise remain closed to you in French. The dictionary gives you columns of expressions with *coup*; let us simply insist on the necessity of learning off the great majority of them and of being able to use them in context, since out of context they can be catastrophic. Think of what the countless uses made of 'get', with or without its postpositions, mean to a foreigner learning English, and you have the idea.

Here are several expressions which you may want to consider more closely:

coup d'œil: *Ça se voit au premier coup d'œil.* 'It is evident at a glance.' *Jeter un coup d'œil sur*: 'to give a quick look at'.

coup de foudre: Most often used to mean 'love at first sight'.

coup de main: 'A hand', 'helping hand'. *Peux-tu venir me donner un coup de main pour tapisser mon salon?* 'Can you come over to give me a hand in papering my living room?'

coup de fil: 'A telephone call'. *Il n'y a qu'à nous donner un coup de fil.* 'All you have to do is give us a ring (call us up).'

sur le coup: 'At first', 'at the time'. *Sur le coup je ne me suis pas rendu compte de ce qui s'était passé.* 'At the time, I scarcely realized what had happened.'

coup d'air. 'Draught', 'chill'. Also, *coup de soleil*, 'sunstroke' or 'sunburn'. Both used with *attraper un. Il a mal à l'œil; il a dû attraper un coup d'air.* 'One of his eyes hurts; he must have caught a chill.' *Elle a attrapé un méchant coup de soleil.* 'She's got severe sunburn.'

coup de fusil. Not only 'a gunshot', but 'an unexpectedly high restaurant *or* hotel bill'.

coup de tête. 'An impulse'; *agir sur un coup de tête*, 'to act impulsively'.

à chaque coup, à tous les coups: 'Every time.' Synonymous with *à chaque fois*.

donner un coup de balai, peigne, klaxon, de fer, and so on and on. 'To sweep', 'comb', 'honk the horn', 'iron', etc. Literally, 'to give a touch *or* blow of the instrument in question'. An astonishingly common construction, replacing *balayer, peigner, klaxonner, repasser.* . . .

coupable (m). The guilty person; or, as an adjective, 'guilty'. But you may stumble over the noun, 'guilt', which is *la culpabilité*.

coupe-papier (m). 'Letter opener' (*v.* BUREAU). This is as good a time as any to look at the formation of such words, which we may call the compounds of function. This one would be translated literally 'cut-paper'. When you compare it with the English 'paper cutter' (or 'letter opener'), you notice first of all the inversion in the order of noun and verb, and then the fact that the verb (*coupe*) is actually another noun in English: 'cutter'. The rule of verb-plus-object in French is a consistent and useful one. Look at *coupe-légumes* ('vegetable cutter') and all of the *coupe-* words; *presse-papiers* ('paperweight'); *serre-livres* ('book ends'); and especially the long list of words formed with *porte-* (q.v.).

crédit (m). In the singular, this is likely to mean either 'influence': *user de son crédit auprès de quelqu'un*, 'to use one's influence on someone', and *épuiser son crédit*, 'no longer to have any influence' or 'credit'. The plural means 'funds'. *La ville a été obligée d'abandonner ses projets pour le nouveau stade, faute de crédits.* 'The city has been forced to drop its plans for a new stadium, for lack of government allocations (funds).'

crème (m). Yes, masculine, when you mean 'coffee and cream', 'white coffee', ordered at *un café* or *une terrasse. Un express* is ordinary 'black coffee'; and *un filtre*, 'drip coffee'.

crever. This is the word you need when your car begins to bump along suspiciously. *Je crois que j'ai un pneu crevé.* 'I think I've got a flat tire'. 'The puncture' itself is *une crevaison* (*v.* the chapter on LA VOITURE).

If you yourself are *crevé*, you are not 'wounded' but simply 'dead tired'. This is not a very elegant expression but is certainly current enough; similarly, *crever* in the sense of 'to die'.

crise (f). This word may seem to you to crop up everywhere at once, even where English would use 'attack' or 'problem', instead of 'crisis'. *Il se trouve devant une très grave crise de conscience.* 'He is confronted with a most serious moral problem.' *A la suite de la crise ministérielle, la femme du ministre a fait une crise de nerfs et lui a eu une crise cardiaque.* 'After the governmental crisis, the minister's wife went into hysterics and he himself had a heart attack.'

croiser. Here is an alternative to *rencontrer* when you want to say that you ran into someone. *J'ai croisé sa sœur l'autre soir.* 'I bumped into his sister the other evening.' It can also mean 'to pass someone' (with or without seeing him) who is going in the opposite direction. *J'ai dû le croiser en venant.* 'I must have gone past him on my way here'.

crudités (f. pl.). One of the most blunder-engendering of *Faux Amis*. Nothing to do with the crudeness of a person, but among the first items on a menu: 'an assortment of raw vegetables'. *Cru* means 'raw', and does also mean 'crude' when applied to someone's language.

cuivres (m. pl.). 'The brass instruments.' 'The woodwinds' are *les bois*; 'wind instruments' in general are *les instruments à vent*. The other categories of instruments are those *à cordes* and those *de percussion*.

curé (m). Strictly speaking, *le curé* is not 'the curate' but 'the vicar'; and *le vicaire* is not 'the vicar' but 'the curate'.

cure (f). 'A cure', 'a treatment', as at a spa or watering place. But the verb 'to cure' is *guérir*; and 'a cure' in the sense of a recovery is *une guérison*. 'The healer' is *le guérisseur*.

cure-dent (m). Not a cure for aching teeth, but the humble 'toothpick', which serves to *se curer les dents*, 'to clean (by picking) one's teeth'.

D

dactylo (f). A feminine word, though it looks masculine; for *une dactylo* is 'a typist'; and 'a shorthand-typist/secretary' *une sténodactylo*, since *la sténographie* means 'shorthand' or 'stenography'. *Une thèse doit être dactylographiée.* 'A thesis must be typed.' But the machine itself, 'the typewriter', is *la machine à écrire*, and the action of using it is *taper à la machine*.

daltonien. 'Colorblind.' The condition is *le daltonisme*.

d'après. When it means 'according to', this word is used just like *selon. D'après lui, c'est la plus belle ville de France.* 'According to him, it's the loveliest city in France.' *D'après la pendule, il est plus tôt que je ne pensais.* 'According to the clock, it's earlier than I thought.'

It can also be used where *selon* cannot, to mean 'adapted from' or 'based on', also expressed by *adapté de* or *tiré de. Un grand film d'après le célèbre roman de Zola,* 'an important film based on Zola's famous novel'.

débrouiller, se. Beyond the shadow of a doubt, the first word you should learn in French, since without it, you cannot understand the French and their outlook on life. *Se débrouiller* and the justly famous *Système D (le système de la débrouillardise)* express a whole concept, essentially individualistic, which is only very feebly translated by 'to manage', 'to get along', 'to muddle through', 'to make out for oneself'. If you call someone *très débrouillard(e)*, you are paying him one of the highest compliments that the list of French adjectives allows for: it means a compound of *astucieux, énergique, indépendant,* and *volontaire*, not to mention *imaginatif*. To be resourceful all by oneself is the principal idea here.

—*Mais, Monsieur le Directeur, il n'est pas possible de terminer les préparatifs si vite.*—*Je ne veux pas le savoir, débrouillez-vous pour que ce soit fait aujourd'hui en huit.* 'But, sir, it's impossible to get everything ready so fast.'—'That's not my problem, just be sure it is done a week from today.' *Le pauvre garçon ne gagne pas lourd mais il se débrouille quand même.* 'The poor chap doesn't earn much, but he manages all the same.'

débutant. Just a reminder that *un(e) débutant(e)* is 'a beginner' in general, in any field, and that its meaning is not limited to that of the young woman making her entry into society, 'the deb', as in English. The same goes, of course, for *débuter* and *faire ses débuts*.

dégivrer. 'To defrost', as a refrigerator. *Le dégivrage* is 'the defrosting', whereas *un dégel* is 'a thaw' (in the weather or the political climate).

dégustation (f). 'A tasting *or* sampling of food'; often written over *cafés* and *terrasses*. The verb is *déguster*, although the general verb for 'to taste' is *goûter*.

déjà. This is pretty clearcut as the dictionary gives it to you: the adverb meaning 'already'. But you had better learn by heart: *C'est déjà ça!*, and how to use it. *C'est toujours ça* (*de gagné, de pris*, or something along those lines) is a nearly identical twin.
—*Le plombier ne viendra pas avant vendredi, mais il a promis de venir tout au début de la matinée.—Eh bien, c'est déjà ça!* 'The plumber won't come till Friday, but he's promised to come first thing in the morning.—Well, that's something anyhow!'
   As you can see, the idea is one of being resigned to a bad situation and grateful for what help, or money, you can get.

demander, se. Should you wonder how to say 'I wonder', here you are: *je me demande*. 'A wonder', however, is *un miracle* or *une merveille*; and 'Alice in Wonderland' is known as *Alice au Pays des Merveilles*.

démarrer. The verb for starting the car and, very frequently, for starting anything in general. This general sense, although by no means *incorrect*, is inelegant and distinctly *familier*. *Le démarreur* is 'the starter' in the car. *La manivelle* is 'the crank', for those grim moments *quand le démarreur ne fonctionne pas* (*v*. the chapter on LA VOITURE).
   J'ai beaucoup de travail mais je n'arrive pas à démarrer. 'I have loads of work, but I can't seem to get going on it.'

demi (m). 'A beer', as you order it in a café. *Un demi-panaché*, 'beer and *limonade*' (q.v.).—a 'lemonade shandygaff'.

dépanner. The first meaning is to repair what has broken down; *la panne* is 'the breakdown'. *Tomber en panne*, 'to break down'; *être en panne*, 'to have broken down' (*v*. the chapter on LA VOITURE).
   A further, very common meaning is 'to help someone out temporarily', and usually, materially. *Je n'ai plus de sucre, auriez-vous la gentillesse de me dépanner?* 'I've no more sugar, would you be kind enough to let me have some?' *Puisqu'il ne pouvait pas se payer une chambre à l'hôtel, je l'ai dépanné.* 'Since he couldn't pay for a hotel room, I gave him a bed at my place.'

dépayser. Literally, 'to make (someone) feel as though he were in another country'. In fact, the feeling of *dépaysement* (m) can come with the move from one house or neighborhood to another, or even from one atmosphere or décor to another. *De la salle Louis XIII, nous sommes ensuite passés dans une salle fin dix-neuvième: quel dépaysement!* 'On leaving the gallery in Louis XIII style, we entered a late nineteenth-century room: what a change!, *or* all the difference in the world!' *Avec ce changement d'école, mon fils se sent un peu dépaysé.* 'My son has changed schools and feels a bit out of place.' *Que de gens cherchent à se dépayser en lisant!* 'How many people try to find new horizons by reading!'

dépister. A verb to be careful of, since it can have contrary meanings. Most commonly, perhaps, it means 'to track down': *dépister les sources du cancer*, 'to track down (find out) the causes of cancer'. But the same verb can also mean 'to throw off the scent'.

déposer. This is the word you want when you leave something with the *concierge*—a practice which is still widespread and often very convenient. *Je ne peux pas passer prendre le paquet, ayez la gentillesse de le déposer chez ma concierge.* 'I can't come over to pick up the parcel; please be so good as to leave it with the porter.'
   Il a déposé ses bagages à la gare. 'He's left his bags at the station.'
   Déposer quelqu'un is 'to drop someone off' (at his home, at the corner, etc.). But be careful: *déposer un roi* is 'to bring down (dethrone) a king'!

dépression (f). Notice that this is not the word you really want for 'an economic depression' such as that of the 1930's: here, *une récession* is called for, or *une crise économique* or *financière*, or *le Krach*, 'the crash'. While we are on depressing subjects, however, note that *une dépression nerveuse* is 'a nervous breakdown'. If you are feeling only momentarily 'depressed', you are *déprimé*. Something that is 'depressing' is *déprimant*.

déranger. The past particle can mean 'mad' or 'deranged', as in English. But you'll need this verb many more times a day to mean 'to bother', 'to put out' or 'impose upon'. It is often used in the negative, as an expression of polite concern. *Je ne vous dérange pas?* 'I hope I'm not interrupting anything?' *Chut, il ne faut pas déranger ton père, il travaille.* 'Hush, don't bother your father; he's working.' Also, 'to go to the trouble of coming': *il s'est dérangé spécialement pour vous voir.* 'He took the trouble of coming just to see you.'

dérouiller. Distinctly colloquial for 'to beat' or 'thrash'; *une dérouillée* is 'a thrashing'. The strict sense is 'to remove rust'; hence, 'to polish', even figuratively.

desservir. A word worth noticing because from one meaning to another, the prefix *de(s)–*, usually a privative in French as in English, can lose all its weight. *Desservir une table* is 'to un-serve (hence clear) the table'; *desservir quelqu'un*, 'to do some-one a disservice'.

But *desservir* in the context in which you are most likely to encounter it, that of public transport, does not mean the opposite of *servir* at all. *Ce quartier est bien desservi par l'auto-bus*. 'This district has good bus service.' *Les arrêts desservis entre 8h15 et 23h30 sont les suivants*. 'The places at which the bus stops between 8.15 a.m. and 11.30 p.m. are the following.'

deux chevaux (f). Also, written *la 2 CV*: the celebrated '2-horse-power Citroën car', sturdy and relatively cheap.

diapositive (f). 'A color slide' or 'transparency'. You may also hear it called *un diapositif*, or simply *un(e) diapo*.

Dieu. You will find traces of divinity everywhere you go in France, 'the eldest daughter of the Church'. In family names, like *Dieudonné*; in place names, like *Villedieu-les-Poêles*; and in the name of every other *rue* and *place*, where the saints are rivalled only by *le Général Leclerc*, *Gambetta*, *Clémenceau*, *la Résistance*, *la Libération*, *le Général de Gaulle* and, since 1963 of course, *le Président Kennedy*. When it comes to first names, however, you will note that *Jésus* is never given, as it is so commonly in Spanish. Nor are 'the gods' at the theatre called '*les dieux*' but rather, *le paradis* or *le poulailler*.

There is nothing blasphemous about *Mon Dieu!*: 'Oh dear', 'dear me!' and so on, in the same quite innocent vein. *Bon sang!* and especially *Bon Dieu!* are a good deal stronger, however, whereas *Ciel!* sounds a bit too much eighteenth century. The name of the baker at the corner of our street is quite simply *Dieu*—which is a neat reminder that in France, *le restaurant* and *l'Eglise*, *le chef saucier* and *le prêtre*, *la table* and *l'autel* have always been close rivals.

difficilement. A very common adverb, as proven by the number of French people who, when learning English, insist on invent-ing 'difficultly' in place of 'with difficulty', or 'not easily'.

diplôme (m). This is more than the piece of paper or parchment on which it is written that you have graduated from such and such an institution; it is the degree itself. *Pour trouver un poste intéressant, il faut avoir un certain nombre de diplômes*. 'To find a promising job, you have to have several degrees.' To graduate (*or* to be graduated) from the Sorbonne is *être diplômé de la Sorbonne*.

direction (f). The first thing to notice here is that, as a general rule, to ask directions is not *demander des directions*, but *demander des indications* or *demander la route*. *Pardon Monsieur, voulez-vous m'indiquer la route pour Malmaison?* 'Excuse me,

sir, would you please give me directions for Malmaison?'
And 'a good sense of direction' is *un bon sens de l'orientation*.

In a car, *la direction* is 'the steering' (*v.* the chapter on LA
VOITURE).

And although you may not think of it the first time around,
in French you rarely 'conduct' an orchestra (*v.* CONDUIRE);
you 'direct' it. *L'orchestre est placé sous la direction de . . .* or,
l'orchestre sera dirigé par . . . 'The orchestra is (will be) con-
ducted by . . .'

'Directions for use' (or for opening a can, etc.) is *le mode
d'emploi*. With a capital *D*, *la Direction* becomes the upper
echelons of the administration. *Votre demande a été transmise
à la Direction.* 'Your request (*or* application) has been sent
on up to the proper authorities.'

discuter. A verb that needs to be looked at along with *disputer*,
which is likely to be the stronger of the two. *Discuter* can mean
simply 'to discuss', 'to talk (over)', without going so far as to
argue; whereas *disputer* immediately implies at least a heated
discussion. The same distinction may be made between *une
discussion* and *une dispute*. *Disputer quelque chose* is 'to contest
it' or 'to contend for it', from *un prix* to *un match* to *un objet
vendu aux enchères*.

All doubt disappears with *se disputer*, which is 'to have a
falling out', a real difference or quarrel over something. *Quand
je pense que nous nous sommes disputés pour si peu de chose!* 'I
can't believe we actually quarrelled over something so unim-
portant!'

distraire, se. You might not guess that this verb is used as
frequently as *s'amuser* to mean 'to have fun', 'to relax'. *Arrête-
toi donc de travailler, il faut bien se distraire un peu!* 'Leave off
work, you've got to have some fun.' *Une distraction* is 'an
amusement', 'fun'—or else 'absent-mindedness' or the fact
of 'being distracted'. *Il est très distrait*, 'he's very absent-
minded'.

divorcer. You need to pay particular attention to the intransitive
construction that this verb requires: *divorcer d'avec* (or *avec*)
Untel is the only way to say 'to divorce someone'. You may
prefer to get around this form by saying, for instance, *ils sont
divorcés depuis six mois* or again, *ils ont divorcé . . .* , or *le
divorce a été prononcé* (or *obtenu*) *il y a . . .*

dixième (m). We are not calling your attention to the ordinary
ordinal, 'tenth', but to the most common sort of chance you
can buy in the weekly *Loterie Nationale*: a ticket which entitles
you to one tenth of the full stakes if your number comes up.
Of course it costs only one tenth of what a full *billet* does. In
either case, you can buy your *billet* in a *tabac* (q.v.) or from
any of the street-corner booths in which a man (often dis-
abled) or sometimes a woman (usually knitting) sits patiently

all day for the express purpose of selling *des billets de la Loterie.*
Tirage Mercredi or *Tirage Ce Soir* tells you that the drawing
is to be on Wednesday (or tonight). *Gros Lot de 100.000 francs*
announces big stakes of about £7,200, or $20,000.

domestique (m. or f.). 'A servant.' *Les domestiques* or *les gens de
maison* refers to the class as a whole.

donner. One of those verbs which play so active and varying a
part in daily speech. You might pay especial attention to
expressions in which *donner* replaces 'make' in English. *L'air
de la mer donne faim.* 'The salt air makes you hungry.' And the
same goes for 'to make (someone feel) hot, cold, *or* sleepy'.

   Ce n'est pas donné—a phrase which crops up frequently in
these inflationary days—means 'it's not cheap'; in other words,
'it's expensive'.

   Ne rien donner, in regard to an attempt or a manœuvre, can
be translated as 'being of no avail', 'not leading anywhere'.
On a voulu le raisonner, mais cela n'a rien donné. 'They tried to
reason with him, but got nowhere.' *Donner quelque chose*
means, then, 'to lead somewhere', 'give some result'. *Qu'est-
ce-que ça donne?* 'What's the result?'

   Donner raison à quelqu'un means 'to side with someone', 'to
consider that he is right'. *Le patron a donné raison à mon
collègue plutôt qu'à moi, alors, me voilà dehors!* 'The boss
decided my colleague, and not I, was right; so here I am,
out of a job!' And *donner tort*, as you would expect, is 'to
blame someone', or 'to side against him'.

   Donner le change à quelqu'un is one of those elusive phrases
which do not lend themselves to pithy, accurate translations.
You might say 'to hoodwink someone'.

   Watch out for the distinction, apparently troublesome,
between *donner du mal*, 'to be difficult', 'give trouble', and
se donner du mal, 'to go to a lot of trouble'. *Ce travail* (or *cet
enfant*) *me donne du mal.* 'This job (*or* this child) is difficult,
troublesome for me.' *Il se donne du mal pour son travail* (*son
enfant*). 'He goes to a lot of trouble for his job (his child).'

dossier (m). 'A file of records *or* information' on someone or
something. ('A nail file' is *une lime à ongles*.) Also 'the back
of a chair', which you cannot call simply *'le dos'*.

double (m). The word for 'carbon copy' or 'duplicate'. *Vous
voudrez bien me taper ce mémorandum en un original et trois
doubles.* 'Be so good as to type up this memo with three carbon
copies.' The idea of duplication extends to resemblance
between persons. *Chaque personne a son double quelque part
dans le monde.* 'Everyone has a double somewhere in the
world.'

   Une voie à double sens is 'a two-way street', as opposed to
une voie à sens unique ('one-way street') or *à sens interdit* ('no
entry').

Doubler is 'to overtake *or* pass another car'. *Interdit de doubler en virage.* 'No overtaking on corners (no passing allowed on a curve)' (*v.* the chapter on LA VOITURE).

Doubler is also 'to line'; and when you buy a skirt or a suit, you want to make sure whether it is *entièrement doublé*, and to check on the quality of *la doublure*, 'the lining'. *Une enveloppe doublée*, 'a lined envelope'.

Une doublure is also 'the stand-in' or 'understudy' of a cinema star; *se faire doubler*, 'to use a double'. *Doubler*, in cinematic terms, also means 'to dub in sound': *la version doublée*, as opposed to *la version originale*. 'The dubbing' itself is *le doublage*.

Faire double emploi, 'to be redundant *or* superfluous.'

To express the opposite of *double*, in certain contexts where English may require 'single', French may use *simple* (*v.* also ALLER). *Les prix ont augmenté du simple au double.* 'Prices have doubled.'

dragée (f). 'A sugar-coated almond'. Great quantities of them are distributed on the occasion of *un baptême* or *une communion*.

draguer. A verb which may not last but which has come into current use these past few years; by extension of the usual meaning 'to dredge', it means for a young man 'to go out (often in a group) looking for girls'. *Le dragueur* is the fellow who goes out on such a quest, preferably with *une voiture de sport*.

dresser. An unmistakable *Faux Ami*, since it has nothing to do with getting dressed, which is *s'habiller*; nor with dressing someone else, which is *habiller*; nor with 'a dress', *une robe*, nor yet with apparel in general, *les vêtements*. And still less with 'a chest of drawers' (US: 'dresser'), which is *une commode*. The meaning which you most need to remember is that of 'setting up, i.e. establishing, *or* drawing up a document'. *Dresser un bilan* may be translated 'to make a summary'. *Le Président nous a dressé le bilan des activités de la Bourse en 1965.* 'The Chairman summarized the activities of the Stock Exchange in 1965' (*v.* also BROSSER).

Or again, 'to train': *dresser un chien. Le dressage* is 'the training'. Nothing to do with 'the dressing' of a salad, which is *l'assaisonnement*.

droit (m). 'A right', *or* 'the right' of a moral sort. Although 'to be right' is *avoir raison* (and 'to be wrong', *avoir tort*), 'to be in the right *or* within your rights' (in the case of an automobile accident, especially) is *être dans son droit*, just as 'to be in the wrong' is *être dans son tort. Le droit* is also 'the law', 'the legal science'. *La Faculté de Droit* is 'law school'; *un étudiant en droit*, 'a law student'. *La loi* means 'the law' in the sense of a ruling, 'a bill (*un projet de loi*) passed into law'. *Un hors-la-loi*, 'an outlaw'.

'Right' as opposed to 'left' is, of course, *la droite*, as opposed to *la gauche*. *Prenez le premier virage à gauche et vous verrez la Mairie sur la droite* (or *à droite*).   'Take the first turn to the left and you'll see the Town Hall on the right.'

E

échapper. This verb can serve not only where you would instinctively use 'escape' in English—*s'échapper de prison*—but as often where the situation calls for 'let slip', 'overlook', 'elude', 'be beyond (one)'. *Le vase m'a échappé des mains.* 'The vase slipped out of my hands.' *J'avoue bien humblement que le sens de son astuce m'a totalement échappé.* 'I must admit that the meaning of his witticism (sally, joke) was beyond me, *or* escaped me, altogether.' *Il a laissé échapper un gros mot en pleine réunion.* 'Right in the middle of the meeting he let slip a swear word.'

A number of French words take on a special meaning when it comes to automobiles, scooters, or anything motorized: and *le pot d'échappement* is 'the exhaust pipe'.

You may be wondering what separates *s'évader* from (*s'*)*échapper*. When you really mean 'an escape', as from prison, the two are pretty nearly interchangeable. A certain film was titled *La Grande Evasion*; another, however, was called *Un Condamné à Mort S'est Echappé*. Yet the meaning, obviously, is the same in both cases. But as soon as you want any of the figurative meanings given above, *évader* will not do at all.

échéance (f). 'The due date', or 'maturity *or* expiration date' of a bill, a bond, a lease or a permit. But *à brève échéance* (like *à court terme*) and *à longue échéance* (and *à long terme*) have a more common and extended meaning: 'in the short run', and 'in the long run'. The latter can also be expressed simply by *à la longue*.

Bear in mind that this word comes from the verb *échoir*, 'to lapse', 'fall due', etc., and not from *échouer*, whose noun is *échec* (m), 'failure'.

écouteur (m). 'The ear piece' of the telephone receiver. French telephones often come equipped with a second *écouteur* on a separate wire.

éducation (f). One of those subtle global terms, rather like 'breeding' in English, a compound of tact, politeness, delicacy. And so, more often than not, a *Faux Ami*, since 'education' in the English sense is *l'instruction* (f). *La façon dont Untel s'est comporté témoigne d'un manque total d'éducation.* 'The way So-and-So behaved shows a total lack of manners.' None the less, *le Ministère de l'Education Nationale* does mean the Ministry of Education.

égout (m). The humble 'sewer'; or, in the plural, *les égouts*, 'the system of sewerage'. A common feature of French streets is the blackened bundle of burlap laid up against the kerb (US: curb) to absorb or channel the flow into the *bouche d'égouts.*

But with *un égouttoir,* we move out of the streets and straight into the kitchen: this is 'the dish rack' which you place on *la paillasse,* the drain board. *Egoutter la salade* means to hang up the washed lettuce to drain in *un panier à salade* (v. SALADE). A more vigorous school of thought maintains that *le panier* must be shaken; and just before mealtime you will see *la mère de famille* or the eldest child performing this ritual.

électrophone (m). 'A record player' functioning independently of a radio *(un poste de radio)*; whereas *le tourne-disques* has to be hooked up with the radio. *Un pick-up* or *une stéréo* is another term for *un tourne-disques.* 'The turntable' is *le plateau.*

élever. The critical expressions here are *bien élevé* and *mal élevé*: 'well-bred *or* -behaved', and 'ill-bred *or* -behaved'. No dictionary can give you an accurate notion of the concision of these phrases as social judgements upon people, and of the number of times you run into them. *Cette fille est très sympathique, et bien élevée surtout.* 'That's a very nice girl and, above all, she's polite.' *Ce garçon a beau avoir une grand fortune, il est si déplaisant, si mal élevé!* 'That fellow may be as rich as Crœsus, still he's so disagreeable and so rude!'

embarrasser. A reminder that although you may use this verb to mean 'to embarrass', you had better use *gêner* instead. *Je suis très gêné,* 'I'm most embarrassed.' *(Je suis gêné* can also mean 'I'm temporarily hard up for cash'.) *Je suis confus* also means 'I'm most embarrassed'. For 'embarrassing', *délicat* or *gênant* is called for. *C'est très gênant (délicat) de lui demander directement.* 'It's very embarrassing to ask him outright.'

Save *embarrasser* for 'to encumber', 'to place an obstacle'; the same goes, of course, for *embarrassant (les colis embarrassants,* or *encombrants, ne sont pas admis dans les autobus)* and *un embarras.*

embouteillage (m). The all-too-often needed word for 'traffic jam'. *Si tu avais vu l'embouteillage ce soir à la Concorde à l'heure de pointe!* 'You should have seen the traffic jam (bottleneck) during the rush hour this evening in the Place de la Concorde!'

(There is of course a Franglais expression for *l'heure de pointe* or *d'affluence: l'heure du rush . . .*)

Embouteillage does not nor ever will mean any other sort of jam: neither the sort you eat, which is *la confiture,* nor the sort you get into—'a tight spot' or 'a fix'. For the latter there is, as you would expect, a plenitude of expressions: *avoir des ennuis* or, in terms more *familier*, *avoir des pépins*, *être dans le pétrin* (literally, the apparatus for kneading dough), *être dans de beaux draps* (ironic).

embrocation (f). A pharmaceutical term, not at all common, but more so than in English. You're quite safe, however, in saying *un liniment* or *une lotion* instead.

émotion (f). As it is most often used in English, emotion usually equates with 'sentiment' or 'feeling'. In French, the word extends easily to 'excitement' in general. *Que d'émotion(s)!* 'Such excitement!' *Mon fils nous a donné des émotions hier soir: il avait disparu pendant deux heures!* 'My son really gave us a scare last night: he disappeared for two hours!'

Emouvoir, however, is not the same as *exciter*. *Emouvoir* is 'to move' or 'touch', also 'to upset'. *C'était un spectacle des plus émouvants.* 'It was a most moving sight.' *Un(e) émotif (–ve)* is a person who is very sensitive, readily stirred. *Il faut s'y prendre très doucement avec lui, c'est un grand émotif.* 'With him you have to go about things very carefully; he's so easily upset.'

emprunt (m). 'A loan.' In the *bureau de poste*, you often see signs advertising the *emprunt SNCF*, or 'government railway bond issue'; *l'emprunt EDF*, or 'nationalized electricity bond issue', and so on. The verb, *emprunter*, does not mean 'to lend', which is *prêter*, but 'to borrow'; and *un prêt* also means 'a loan'. *Il m'a consenti un prêt de 15.000 frs.* 'He has granted me a loan of 15,000 francs.' *Il aurait emprunté à Balzac cet art du portrait.* 'His mastery of character description is said to have been modelled on Balzac's'—and notice the construction of the verb: *emprunter à*, 'to borrow from'.

Emprunter can also mean 'to make use of', 'avail oneself of'; and again you can see government posters, *Empruntez les transports publics*: 'Avail yourself of public transport.' The verb here is transitive.

Emprunter une fausse route, or *piste*, 'to go off on the wrong track'.

en. A pretty straightforward item of grammar, you say, and so it is. But by making it precede various verbs, you can change their meaning as radically as you can with postpositions in English. For instance: *En venir là* (or *à cela*), 'to sink that low', 'to come to that'. *Je n'aurais jamais pensé qu'il en serait venu là.* 'I'd never have thought he would come to that.'

En être là, 'to be at . . .' as in *Où en êtes-vous?* 'Where are you at?' ('How far have you got?'). *Voilà où nous en sommes.* 'Here is as far as we've got.' *A propos de votre demande de permis, dites-moi ce qu'il en est.* 'Tell me what's happened to your application for a license.'

S'en prendre à quelqu'un, 'to turn against someone', 'hold something against him', or 'to take it out on him'.

S'en faire, 'to worry'. *Ne vous en faites pas.* 'Don't worry (about it).'

encore. The first thing to notice is that the word is not used as a noun in French the way it is, in a sort of reverse Franglais, by English-speaking people at the end of a concert or recital. Where you may shout 'Encore!', the Frenchman shouts *Bis! Le soliste a eu quinze rappels.* 'The soloist was called back fifteen times.'

. . . *Et encore!* is worth your attention. In a tone of anger or indignation, it means, like *mais encore!*, 'so what?' 'what of it?' But uttered with a philosophical sigh, it signifies 'and even so, that may not be the case'; 'and even then'; and so on. *Madame, le travail de votre fils est tout juste acceptable, et encore.* 'Madam, you son's performance is barely sufficient, and even at that . . .'

enfin. The chief meaning of this adverb is certainly clearcut: 'finally'. But as it is used in daily speech, it can be elusive. Often it rectifies or qualifies what has just been said. *Oh je le déteste! Enfin, je ne l'aime guère.* 'I hate him! I mean, I don't like him at all.' *Il répète toujours la même chose . . . enfin, très souvent.* 'He's forever saying the same thing . . . well, very often anyhow.'

Or again, you may be arguing (amiably) with someone and, exasperated, you cry *mais enfin!*, meaning 'oh, for heaven's sake!', or 'now look here!' or whatever you tend to say under such circumstances. *Mais enfin! où voulez-vous en venir?* 'But what on earth are you trying to get at?' (For another meaning of *en venir, v.* EN.)

ennuyer. 'To bore'. Also, 'to bother *or* embarrass', as in *Ça m'ennuie (C'est très ennuyeux) de lui demander de me rendre ce service.* 'I feel very awkward (embarrassed) about asking him to do me this favor.'

en plus. Literally, 'in addition', as opposed to *compris*, 'included'. *Le prix du volume est de 9F90, taxes locales en plus.* 'Each volume costs 9F90, plus local taxes.' *Menu à 8F: hors d'œuvre, plat de viande, dessert; boisson en plus. Service 15% non compris.* 'Tip of 15%, extra.'

en principe. Impossible to get through the day without making use of this most exasperating, most elastic of expressions. Of course it means 'as a rule', 'in theory'; but no words can convey the infinite scepticism that accompanies it, the shrug of the shoulder, the lift of the eyebrow. The implication of complicity may be very strong. *En principe, elle vient dîner chez nous ce soir; mais tu la connais, je dis bien—en principe.* 'She's supposed to have dinner with us tonight but you know what she's like; she's *supposed* to come.'

en sus. May replace *en plus* (q.v.) on the menu. You'll virtually never find it anywhere else.

entendre parler. When someone asks you pointblank, *avez-vous lu ce livre?* and you want to say 'no, but I've heard of it', then this is the expression to fall back on: *non, mais j'en ai entendu parler. On n'entend parler que de La Callas en ce moment.* 'You hear of no one but Maria Callas these days.'

Entendu, meaning 'all right', 'it's agreed', is generally preferable to *d'accord*, which corresponds to 'OK'. *D'acc* is really too limp to be anything more than slangy. *OK* (pronounced as in English) has been adopted by a good number of French people anxious to sound up to date.

S'entend is not to be confused with *sous-entendu*, although they may seem to you interchangeable. The first is quite like *bien entendu*, *bien sûr*: 'of course', 'it goes without saying'; it stresses an already apparent meaning. But *un sous-entendu* points to 'an implied *or* hidden meaning'. *Son style devient obscur à force de sous-entendus.* 'His style is quite obscure, you have to read so much between the lines.'

entorse (f). If you are so unfortunate as to sprain your ankle, this is the word that applies: *j'ai une entorse à la cheville.* Figuratively, a minor departure from the law or from the truth calls for the same expression. *Son action est une entorse au règlement.* 'His action is a slight deviation from the law'.

Entrez! Just a reminder that when you want to tell the person knocking at the door to come in, this is the expression you need. You cannot use *en avant!*, although an analogy with the Italian may be tempting.

espace (m). The first thing to notice is the masculine gender, since *race* and *place* might lead you to suppose that *espace* too was feminine. Next, there is the difference between *l'espace* and *la place*. *Espace* is simply less tangible, let us say, or less earthly: *l'exploration de l'espace*, 'exploration of (interplanetary) space'. 'Space ship', *engin spatial*. Words or objects which are *espacés* are those arranged with intervals between them. *Ses visites se sont espacées.* 'His visits became more and more infrequent (there was a longer interval between visits).' City planners talk about *les espaces verts*, 'open areas' or 'green spaces'.

La place means 'room' or 'seat': *Cette place est-elle libre, s'il vous plaît?* 'Is this seat free?' (in the train, cinema, etc.). The Mad Hatter and his friends, had they spoken French, would have cried *Plus de place, plus de place!* 'No room, no room!' In the plural, *plus de places* means 'no more seats'.

Louer une place is 'to buy a ticket' for a play or concert.

And of course *une place* is also 'a public square'.

essentiel (m). 'The important thing', 'the main thing' (which you may at first be tempted to translate literally *la chose importante*).

Dites-lui ce que vous voulez, l'essentiel c'est de le voir aujourd'hui.
'Say what you like to him, the main thing is to see him today.'
Le tout and *le principal* are also used in this way.

étanche. The word for 'watertight'; *l'étanchéité* (f) is the noun.
Not to be confused with *imperméable*, 'waterproof', and
imperméabilité (f), the corresponding noun. *Un imperméable* is
'a raincoat' or 'mac'. When you take it to be cleaned you may
need to specify whether you want it merely *nettoyé*, 'cleaned',
or *réimperméabilisé*, 'waterproofed', as well.

étrennes (f. pl.). A word virtually never found in the singular. It
brings up the whole question of New Year's gifts. Christmas
presents, especially for the children, are much more the thing
now than they used to be. But *les étrennes* are still an important
feature, and may be given either on 31 December (*la Saint-
Sylvestre*) or on 1 January. This is the traditional moment for
remembering—with an appropriate sum of money, the calcula-
tion of which is a very subtle business—the people who have
served you throughout the year: the *concierge* and *le facteur*
('postman') are the most obvious examples. Even if you move
into your new flat on New Year's Eve, a rather common time
for doing so in fact, you will do well to give *des étrennes* to
your new *concierge*, and of course you must not forget the old
one when you move out. (*v.* also POURBOIRE). *Etrenner quelque
chose* is 'to use something (especially clothing) for the first
time'.

évolué(e) Another of those terms of social judgement (*v.* also
ÉLEVER), so handy and so critical, which might not occur to
you immediately. You can apply it (*a*) to a whole people, as
you can the verb in English and in which case you would
translate by 'very civilized', 'advanced', 'refined', but probably
not by 'evolved'. (Bear in mind that here we are using the
word as an adjective, a use which is scarcely possible in
English.) Or (*b*) to an individual or individuals, in which case
'enlightened' or 'refined' is perhaps the best translation.

examen (m). The ordinary 'examination', as distinct from *un
concours* (q.v.). *Passer un examen* is the standard way of saying
'to sit for an exam' (US: 'to take an exam'). But 'to pass
an exam'—to come out of it successfully—must be translated
réussir un examen or *être reçu à un examen*. If the case is
unfortunately the opposite, then you have a handful of
expressions from which to choose: *échouer à l'examen* or, more
commonly, *être recalé*; or in terms still more authentically
estudiantins, louper or *rater son examen* or *être collé*. 'The
examiner', except in the case of a medical exam, is *l'examina-
teur*; note the extra syllable.

expérience (f). A notorious traitor of a word; not only 'experience', as in English, but also 'experiment'. You cannot wish
the word *'un expériment'* into existence, although you do have

expérimental, and *expérimentateur* (another case of the extra syllable). And to compound the confusion, the word for 'experienced' is *expérimenté*. This is not so complicated as it sounds, but it does take some getting used to. The word *expérience* by itself—as in *mes expériences en Russie*—could be interpreted to mean *expérience sexuelle*. You had better say *ce qui m'est arrivé en Russie*.

Tenter une expérience is either 'to do an experiment' or 'to attempt something', 'to give it a try.'

exprès. *Faire quelque chose exprès* is the most common way of saying 'to do something deliberately, *or* on purpose'. And of course you can replace *faire* with any other appropriate verb: *elle est venue exprès, il a plongé exprès, je m'en vais exprès*, and so forth.

extra. Not 'extraneous', which is *superflu*; nor 'additional', which is *en plus* or *supplémentaire*; but 'extraordinary', 'exceptionally good'. A bit *familier*. The butcher will often mark his 'top quality roastbeef': *rosbif extra*.

F

façon (f). 'Fashion' in the sense of 'way' or 'manner', or of 'craftsmanship'. But it does not mean 'dress fashion', which is *la mode*.

D'une façon comme d'une autre: literally, 'anyhow', 'at any rate'.

A sa façon, 'in his (her) own way', can be used as a back-handed compliment. *Il était très aimable—enfin, à sa façon.*

(*v*. also: SANS FAÇON.)

faire-part (m). An announcement of a birth, death, or marriage; 'to announce something' is *faire part de quelque chose. Il m'a fait part de ses projets de mariage.* 'He told me of his plans for getting married.'

faisan (m). Can mean, like *faiseur* (m), 'a shark' or 'shady business-man', although the basic meaning is 'pheasant'. *Une faisanderie* is a place where pheasants are bred; cf. *la rue de la Faisanderie* in Paris, very chic.

fait. Or *bien fait*: said of a cheese that is ripe. *Mûr* applies to ripe fruit, vegetables and even, figuratively, to people, but will not do for cheeses. Familiarly, *être (re)fait* is like *se faire avoir*: 'to be had', 'to be duped'.

falloir. This being an impersonal verb, you will hear it most often in the form of *il faut*. (*Il vous faut travailler davantage*; or *il faut que vous travailliez davantage.* 'You have to, *or* must, work more.') But that is no reason for confusing it with *fauter*, which is a different matter altogether: 'to sin' (as used by a priest in confession), 'to be seduced'.

Il faut ce qu'il faut is one of those marvellously concise, untranslatable expressions: 'It takes what it takes.' Said on an occasion requiring an all-out effort to do justice to it, as when *dragées* (q.v.) are distributed to friends on the occasion of *un baptême* or *une communion*.

farces et attrapes (f. pl.). Often used to indicate the whole range of practical jokes, tricks, hoaxes, gadgets to fool people. *La farce* is also 'a (culinary) stuffing'; and the verb, *farcir*, applies only to stuffing. 'To play a practical joke' is *faire une farce (à quelqu'un)*.

farfelu. Means 'bizarre', 'whimsical', 'fanciful', 'exaggerated'. This adjective and its corresponding noun, *le farfelutisme*, are still overlooked by most dictionaries. *J'ai rencontré un camarade que j'avais perdu de vue: toujours aussi farfelu.* 'I ran into an old friend I'd lost track of; just as light-headed and wacky as ever.'

fariboles (f. pl.). 'Fiddlesticks!', 'nonsense'. (*v.* BONIMENT.)

faubourg (m). This word would seem gradually to be giving way to *la banlieue*—'suburbs' or 'outskirts'—but may still be used to mean 'an outlying and humble neighborhood of working-class population'. An apparently contradictory connotation of aristocracy attaches to the old *Faubourg St. Germain* which, like the present *rue du Faubourg St. Honoré*, is now not only within the gates of Paris, but right in the center and one of the most sought-after quarters.

faux frais (m. pl.). These are incidentals, the items which you are prone to forget in making out your budget—*les taxis, les pourboires, les fleurs pour votre hôtesse, les timbres-poste, et le reste!*

férié. *Un jour férié* is 'a holiday', as opposed to *un jour ouvrable*, or 'working day' when shops, banks, and the like are open. *Le lundi de la Pentecôte est un jour férié.* 'The Monday after Whitsun is a holiday.'

ferme (f). 'A farm'; but whereas in English you live 'on a farm', in French you live 'in' it: *dans la ferme*, or *à la ferme*.

As an adjective, *ferme* has, among others, a meaning which may not appear in the dictionary. *Il fut condamné à trois ans de prison ferme.* 'He was sentenced to three years' imprisonment.' As opposed to: *Il fut condamné à trois ans de prison avec sursis.* 'He was given a three-year suspended sentence.'

If you want the word for 'a firm' or 'business', then you mean not *ferme* but *firme* (f); at all events, by far the commoner term for it is *une société (anonyme)*.

fermeture annuelle (f). A fact of commercial life which has attained the proportions of a national phenomenon; virtually every *boutique* or *magasin* (except *les grands magasins*, or 'department stores') and many restaurants and theatres will close for the month of August. Beginning usually in mid-June an announcement of the dates of its *fermeture* is tacked to every shop door or chalked on the windows. For the few Parisians who remain in Paris during this singular month, there is the joy of being able to drive and park their cars with relative ease, countered by the problem of finding *une boulangerie, une crémerie, une boucherie, une blanchisserie*, even *un tabac* open in the neighborhood. The government is making vigorous efforts to persuade people to stagger their holidays (*v.* CONGÉ) over the period from June to September, particularly since *la rentrée*—'the re-opening of schools'— does not come much before the end of September. But August remains the height of the season *au bord de la mer*—and of the tourist season in Paris.

fermeture éclair (f). 'A zipper'. A trade name (*v.* BIC). 'A snap fastener' for clothing is *un bouton-pression*.

fête (f). 'Holiday', in general (although 'to go on holiday' is *partir en vacances*). But *les fêtes*, or *la période des fêtes*, refers almost exclusively to the Christmas-and-New-Year's season. *Sa fête* is 'one's saint's day' or 'name-day'; *son anniversaire*, 'one's birthday'. *Fêter son anniversaire*, 'to celebrate one's birthday'.

feu (m). Doubtless you already know that when you want to ask for a light for your cigarette, you cannot request *une lumière, une flamme*, nor anything but *du feu: avez-vous du feu? Une allumette* of course is 'a match'; *un briquet*, 'a cigarette lighter'; *un cendrier*, 'an ashtray'; *un porte-cigarettes*, 'a cigarette case' (*v.* PORTE).
   Faire du feu is 'to light a fire' or 'to heat' one's house. *Le temps est si doux que je n'ai pas fait de feu.* 'The weather is so mild that I haven't turned on the heat in (bothered to heat) my house.'
   Mettre le feu, however, is 'to set fire to' something. *Attention où tu poses ton fer à repasser, tu vas mettre le feu.* 'Be careful where you put your iron; you'll set the house on fire.'
   Les feux are 'traffic lights'. *Le feu vient de passer au vert.* 'The light has just turned green' (*v.* the chapter on LA VOITURE).

figuratif. If you're talking about art, this is the translation of 'figurative'. But 'a figurative meaning' is *un sens figuré*—as opposed to 'literal meaning', *le sens propre*—and 'figuratively' is *au sens figuré*. 'A figure of speech', however, is *une façon de parler*. *Façon de parler* said as a sort of afterthought, means 'as it were', or 'so to speak'.

figurer, se. A much more common means than you might imagine of expressing 'to know', 'to imagine'. *Figurez-vous que je l'ai vu hier?* 'Did you know that I saw him yesterday?'

filer. 'To run' or 'ladder', when it comes to stockings. And 'to disappear rapidly' when it comes to persons, time, or money. *Filer à l'anglaise* is 'to take French leave'.

fille (f). The thing to steel yourself to from the beginning is that there seems to be no age limit for calling a female *une fille*; and that the term in itself need have neither infantile nor dubious connotations (although *aller voir les filles* does distinctly mean 'to go to a brothel'). A woman of 75 may well call her contemporary *une fille: c'est une brave fille*. Clearly there is no disrespect implied here; but for a woman of 20 to call the same person *une fille*, unthinkable. Since the line is so hard to draw, it all being a matter of context and *milieu*, you will do well to say *une femme, une jeune femme, une femme d'un certain âge* (roughly, 'middle-aged'), or *une dame* for an older respected woman, at least until you are certain whom you're talking about and to whom. For a female of your own age or less, there is no problem (*v.* also GARÇON).

Une vieille fille* is 'an old maid', although politeness would call for *une femme célibataire*.
Une amie, or *une petite amie*, 'girl friend'.
Le nom de jeune fille, 'maiden name'.

flacon (m). 'A small bottle' or 'flask', particularly for medicines and perfume. You would never say *une bouteille* in speaking of either of those items, any more than you would speak of '*un flacon' de vin*.

flotter. A colloquial way of saying *pleuvoir*, just as *la flotte* can replace *la pluie*, but as a general rule you will do better to use the more classic terms. *Il n'est pas tombé de la dernière pluie* means 'he was not born yesterday'.

foncièrement. 'Basically', 'profoundly'; and more widely used than you might expect, judging from the rather restricted sound of *foncier*, 'landed', as in *crédit foncier*. *Il faut se méfier de cet homme, il cache bien son jeu mais il est foncièrement méchant*. 'Beware of that man, he's thoroughly bad but he knows how to cover it up.'

fond (m). *Au fond* is a handy little phrase corresponding to 'come to think of it', or 'when you come right down to it', or 'at bottom.' *Un fond* is 'a background' (as in painting) and *au fond de la salle* is 'at the back of the room'.

forcément. A more commonly used adverb than you might think, for 'necessarily'. *Vous qui êtes français, vous connaissez tous les fromages.—Pas forcément!* 'Since you are French, you must be familiar with every sort of cheese.' 'Not necessarily!' Similarly, *c'est forcé* is very often employed to mean 'it's unavoidable', 'it's necessarily so', and *ce n'est pas forcé* to mean the contrary (*v.* also OBLIGATOIRE).

forme (f). *Etre en forme* is a most convenient expression for 'to be in good shape, feeling well'. *Allez donc au théâtre sans moi, je ne me sens pas très en forme.* 'Go on to the theatre without me; I'm not really feeling up to snuff.' *Elle est en pleine forme.* 'She's just fine.' 'A form', in the sense of a standard or official document, is *un formulaire—le formulaire de demande de la carte de séjour,* 'the application form for a residence permit' —or simply *une feuille. Il faut remplir les feuilles d'impôts avant le 4 mars.* 'Tax forms must be filled out by 4 March.'

four (m). Not only 'oven', but 'a failure' or 'flop' as well. In the latter meaning it cannot be applied to persons, however: only to plays, music, books, any sort of performance or entertainment.

fourneau (m). 'A furnace', as you would expect; but also 'a stove' or 'cooker'. 'A furnace' is also termed *une chaudière,* especially when placed in your own flat for individual central heating. 'A stove' is more commonly called *une cuisinière (électrique* or *à gaz),* a word which in turn can also mean 'a cook'. Which is why many a Frenchman, translating literally, may call your cook 'a cooker'.

'The bowl' of a pipe is, again, *un fourneau;* 'the stem' is *le tuyau.*

franc (m). Since 1960, what was first called *'le nouveau franc'* and is now *'le franc'* has officially replaced what was previously *100 anciens francs,* and *le centime* has replaced the former *ancien franc.* In other words, the pair of shoes which cost *69 francs 99 centimes* today would, in 1959, have cost *6.999 anciens francs.* The *ancien franc,* which remains for most Frenchmen today the authentic if unofficial way of counting, is also officially termed *le franc léger,* as compared to the *(nouveau) franc* or *franc lourd.* If you are writing a check for that pair of shoes, you write it, of course, in the official way: *soixante-neuf francs et quatre-vingt-dix-neuf centimes.*

Être franc (–che), 'to be frank'.

Avoir son franc-parler, 'to be outspoken', 'not to mince one's words'.

frapper. A verb that crops up in a handful of everyday contexts. *Entrez sans frapper* on the door of some administrative office enjoins you to 'enter without knocking'. *Tiens! on frappe:* 'I say, there's someone at the door'. 'I hear someone knocking': *J'entends frapper.*

Frapper also has the more forceful meaning 'to strike'. First of all, physically: *il a frappé le cambrioleur.* 'He struck the burglar.' *Ce qui m'a surtout frappé, c'est la propreté de son intérieur.* 'I was especially struck by the spotlessness of his home.' *Il y a une ressemblance frappante entre l'oncle et le neveu.* 'There is a striking resemblance between uncle and nephew.' *On va frapper une nouvelle pièce de 10 francs.* 'They're going to mint a new 10 franc piece.'

Frapper le vin (blanc), 'to chill (white) wine'.

froid (m). As a noun, *le froid* does mean 'the cold'—in terms either of weather or of refrigeration. But 'a cold', the sneeze and cough variety, is *un rhume*, and 'to have a cold' is *être enrhumé*; 'to have a bad cold', *être très enrhumé* or *avoir un gros rhume*. Whereas 'to catch a cold' is *attraper un rhume*, 'to catch cold' is *attraper* or *prendre froid*.

froisser. 'To crumple' or 'wrinkle'; and 'to ruffle' in a figurative way, 'to offend', which you can also express by *offenser*, of course. 'To hurt *or* wound (someone's feelings)' is *blesser*, which may also mean, 'to inflict a physical wound'. *Mais ne te froisse pas! je te dis ce que je pense, voilà tout!* 'Don't get your back up! I'm just telling you what I think.'

Un tissu infroissable (or *indéformable*) is 'wrinkleproof cloth'.

fumiste. An elusive adjective (or noun), implying an inclination both to practical jokes and to laziness and daydreaming. A close cousin of *un farceur* and *un plaisantin*, as in *un joyeux fumiste*.

If you have a fireplace, you will require the services of a professional *fumiste*, who is, on the contrary, a very serious person indeed, his business being *la fumisterie*, 'the repairing of stoves and chimneys'. *Un ramoneur* is the man who cleans them, 'a sweep'.

fusionner. This is the verb you want in talking of a merger between two companies (*sociétés*; *v.* S.A.). 'The merger' itself is *la fusion*.

G

gâchis (m). From the verb *gâcher*. Quite a common, and strong word for 'a mess'—different from *un fatras* in that *un gâchis* is not only disorder but a mess caused by bungling and ineptness.

gaffe (f). 'A boat hook', certainly; but far more frequently, 'a social blunder', like *une bévue* or *un faux pas*. *Il a fait une gaffe énorme*. 'He made a terrific blunder.' *Faire gaffe*, however, without the indefinite article, is a very colloquial phrase: 'to be careful', 'to pay attention'. *Alors, faites gaffe à la différence entre ces deux expressions!*

galette (f). On 6 January, or Twelfth Night, it is the custom to '*tirer les rois*': you buy a round flat flaky cake, *la galette* (*fourrée aux amandes*, or not), with which the *boulangerie* will usually furnish a gilt-paper crown. The person who finds the little plastic king in his portion of *galette* is the king (or queen), and has the right to choose his queen (or her king).

This is a very pleasant little ceremony, reserved for the family or close friends.

In slang, *la galette*, like *le fric*, means 'money'.

gant de toilette (m). Also called *une main de toilette*. 'A wash-cloth' which instead of being a flat square, is sewn up to form an oblong glove. It is made of *tissu éponge* ('towelling *or* terry cloth'), just like 'a bath towel' (*une serviette éponge*).

garage (m). On certain little-frequented and excessively narrow roads in Provence, the word will indicate a modest lay-by at the edge where you can pull off to let a car go by in the opposite direction. Otherwise, however, the word means, as in English, 'a repair shop' or 'a closed space for parking your car' (*v.* BOX). Notice that you put your car *au garage*, and not '*dans le*' *garage*.

garce (f). One of the nastier epithets applicable to the female of the species: 'a bitch', no less. So beware, and for heaven's sake don't think that it means 'a tomboy'! More than one person has been known (and what is worse, heard) to fall prey to that confusion. 'A tomboy' is simply *un garçon manqué*.

garçon (m.). The same remark as for *fille* (q.v.): no apparent age limit. *C'est un brave garçon.* 'He's a fine chap (nice fellow).' Again, to be on the safe side in speaking, you will do well to say *un homme*, *un jeune homme*, *un homme d'un certain âge* or more respectfully, *un monsieur*. The maid, when you come home and ask her for messages, will say, not *un garçon*, but *un monsieur a téléphoné.*

By analogy with *une vieille fille*, *un vieux garçon* is 'a bachelor', especially a confirmed one; again, a more courteous term is *un célibataire. Enterrer sa vie de garçon*, 'to have a last fling with the boys before marrying'.

And no matter what his age, 'the waiter' in a restaurant or at *une terrasse* is *le garçon*; to summon him you call *Garçon!*, and not *Monsieur.*

Un garçon de courses is 'an errand boy', otherwise called *un coursier* (just like a horse—in more poetical terms).

gare (f). This is one of the two sorts of *gare*, as you are probably aware: the 'station' or 'terminal' sort. *L'aérogare* is 'the air terminal' (*des Invalides* in Paris), as distinct from *l'aéroport*, 'the airport' (*Orly* or *Le Bourget* in Paris).

The other sort of *gare*, being exclamatory, has no gender. *Gare à vous!* 'Beware!' 'Watch out!' or, in a threatening way, 'I warn you!' *Ma belle-mère est arrivée hier sans crier gare.* 'My mother-in-law arrived yesterday without any warning.'

garer, se. 'To park one's car.' But parking itself is *le stationnement*; *stationnement interdit*, 'no parking'.

gars (m). The dictionary will tell you that this means 'a young fellow'; but the implication if you call someone *un gars* is distinctly one of a superior speaking to (or of) an inferior or, just possibly, one of great familiarity among equals. *Allez les gars!* could be rendered 'come on, boys!' 'let's go, gang!' or some such phrase. The pronunciation calls for a barely audible *r* and a totally inaudible *s*; otherwise you'll find yourself saying *garce* (q.v.).

gâteau (m). 'Cake'—except fruitcake (*v.* CAKE). *Un gâteau sec*, like *un biscuit*, is 'a sweet biscuit' (US: 'cookie'), while *un gâteau salé* is 'a cheese or cocktail biscuit (US: cracker).'

Un papa (or *une maman*) *gâteau* is 'a doting parent'; the verb, *gâter*, is 'to spoil'. *Un enfant gâté*, 'a spoiled child'.

A near-slang expression is *c'est du gâteau*: 'it's as easy as pie', 'it's like falling off a log', 'it's a walkaway'.

gendre (m). 'Son-in-law.' Used alternatively with *beau-fils* (m). Not to be confused with *genre* (m), q.v.

genre (m). 'Gender', 'sort', 'manner', 'type', hence, 'style' as well. *Ça m'étonne de lui, ce n'est pas son genre.* 'I'm surprised at him; that's not at all like him.' *C'est ce qu'on fait de mieux dans ce genre.* 'It's the best thing of its type that you can find.'

Un genre de, or *une sorte de*, may be used and over-used in as meaningless a way as 'a kind of' or 'a sort of' in English.

gens (m. and f. pl.). Lest we forget the classic confusion between *gens* and *peuple*: *les gens* means 'people'; and *le peuple*, 'a people' in the anthropological or political sense. *Les peuples de ce continent*, 'the peoples of this continent'. *Les gens de ce quartier*, 'the people in this neighbourhood'. *En appeler au peuple* is a way of saying 'to bring a question before the voters in a referendum', 'to appeal (or go) to the people'.

The singular of *gens* is *la gent* (both pronounced like the masculine name *Jean*), from the Latin *gens*, nomin., and *gentem*, accus. *La gent* carries a literary meaning, tinged with irony as in La Fontaine: *la gent marécageuse*, 'frogs'; or *la gent épicière*, 'grocers'. The archaic adjective, *gent(e)*, meant 'well-born': *gente dame*, 'gentlewoman'.

goûter (m). Written just like the verb from which it comes, 'to taste'. It approximates to the English custom of afternoon tea, being a snack taken in the late afternoon,[1] but almost always it is for school-children, at about 4 or 4.30, when the schools let out. Which is why it is often called *un quatre heures*. At this time there will be a rush to the nearest *boulangerie* or *pâtisserie* to buy *un petit pain au chocolat* (a soft roll with chocolate tucked inside), *un croissant, un chausson aux pommes*, or simply bread.

It is amazing the number of people, and not only children either, you can see walking about *à l'heure du déjeuner, du goûter*, or *du dîner*, nibbling away at one end of the *baguette* (*v.* PAIN) they've just bought for the approaching meal. So

[1] A morning snack is *un casse-croûte*, which is also any quick light meal.

if you send someone out to buy bread, you will do well to order one bigger than you really need, to allow for its shrinkage on the way home!

Goûter is not to be confused with *goutter*, 'to drip'; *une goutte* is 'a drop'.

graisse (f). 'The fat' or 'grease' used in cooking or resulting from cooking, whereas *le gras* is the fatty part of the meat itself.

La graisse can also be any sort of grease, such as that used on machinery; and *le graissage* is the lubrication done on a car.

Cheese or cream marked 60% *M.G.* (*matières grasses*) has a fat content of 60%. To indicate, on the contrary, that they have a low fat content or none at all, yogurts and certain cheeses will be marked *maigre*. *Faire maigre* is 'to abstain from eating meat', as on Fridays or fast days; *faire gras* is of course not so much to eat fat as 'to eat meat'.

Finally where you may call a dish *gras*—'fatty' or 'heavy' —beware of calling it *graisseux*, which means downright 'greasy'!

And if you ask *le pharmacien* for 'cough syrup', he's likely to ask whether you have *une toux sèche* or *une toux grasse*—'a dry *or* a loose cough'.

grève (f). 'A labor strike'; *la grève générale*—no difficulty in understanding this, surely; the difficulty lies in putting up with it, as it affects all public transport and utilities. *Faire la grève* is 'to go out on strike'; (*être*) *en grève*, '(to be) on strike'. And 'the striker' is *le gréviste*.

La grève in the sense of 'shore' is used for the most part in poetry, rather like 'strand'. It is often applied to that part of the Norman coast nearest to *le Mont St. Michel*.

Etre grevé d'impôts is something else again: 'to be burdened with taxes', so that *être dégrevé d'impôts* is a far more pleasant expression: 'to be relieved from taxes'.

griller. 'To grill' or 'toast'—and 'to overheat', 'to use up by over-heating', as in *griller le moteur, griller la résistance* (*électrique*). *Le pain grillé*, made in *un grille-pain*, or in the oven, is 'toast'; but it is often considered chic to talk of *des toasts*, rounds of pre-toasted bread.

grognon. From *grogner*, 'to growl' or 'snarl'; and said of someone, especially a child, who is grumpy or cranky.

gros mot (m). Not a 'big word', but a 'bad word', or 'swear word' (*juron*, m).

grossir. 'To gain, *or* put on, weight'. You can also say *prendre du poids*. 'To lose, *or* take off, weight': *maigrir*. *Actuellement elle suit un régime rigoureux pour maigrir*. 'Now she's following a strict slimming diet'.

H

habile. 'Skilful', 'able'. You can apply this to something abstract
—*un habile jeu de mots,* 'a clever (*or* agile) play on words'—
as well as to material circumstances. *Elle est très habile de ses
doigts.* 'She is really clever with her hands.'

habillé. Not only 'dressed', but also 'dressy'. *Moi, à ta place, ma
chère, je prendrais ce manteau-là; il est infiniment plus habillé.*
'If I were you, my dear, I'd buy that coat; it's much the more
dressy.' *Un déshabillé* is 'a negligee'. You need to be careful,
by the way, about using the adjective *négligé*; it is not necessarily derogatory. *Elle reçut son amie en négligé.* 'She was
casually dressed when her friend came in.' But: *On le remarqua
au négligé de sa tenue.* 'He stood out by the carelessness of his
appearance.'

hausse (f). The contrary of *la baisse,* in financial and commercial
matters. *Les loyers sont en hausse.* 'Rents are going up.'
La hausse des prix, 'the rise in prices'. *Baisse importante sur le
veau* at the butcher's: 'a big reduction in the price of veal'.
    Hausser les épaules, 'to shrug one's shoulders'. 'The shrug'
itself, however, is not *la hausse* but *le haussement d'épaules.*

histoire (f). Another of those words the correct and frequent use
of which marks the speaker of genuine French. You know that
it means 'history': *l'histoire des pays d'Europe centrale*; and
'story' or 'tale': *une histoire pour enfants. Il raconte des histoires drôles comme personne.* 'He tells funny stories better than
anyone else.'
    But you will also find it meaning 'cock and bull story',
'fuss', 'trouble', 'matter', 'business'. *Ce n'est pas la première
fois qu'il a des histoires avec la police.* 'It's not the first time he's
had a run-in with the police.' *Ne me racontez pas d'histoires.*
'Don't hand me a lot of guff (give me a lot of bull)' (*v.* also
BARATIN). *Toute cette histoire me retourne.* 'The whole business
upsets me.' *Ils m'en ont fait des histoires avant de m'accorder ce
certificat!* 'They made such a fuss before giving me this
reference!'

hôtel particulier (m). This cannot be translated as 'a private
hotel', but as 'a town house'. Many of the finer ones in Paris
have been restored and are open to the public; a number of
them have been taken over by ministries, embassies, or schools.
Very few are still used as town houses.

housse (f).   'A slipcover', over car seats, armchairs, and
the like, or mounted as a movable wardrobe. Or a protective
soft bag to cover, for instance, *un aspirateur* ('vacuum cleaner'),

as opposed to *un étui*, a small rigid case enclosing an easily portable object, as *un étui à lunettes*, or *un écrin*, 'a jewel case'.

Une housse belongs to the relatively small number of words beginning with '*un* h *aspiré*'—so that you say *la housse*, and not '*l'housse*'. *La honte, les Halles, le héron, la hotte, la haine, la hauteur, la hausse, le haricot, la halte,* and *le hasard* are others in this select group.

I

ignorer. Used as often as a phrase which an English speaker finds more likely: *ne pas savoir. J'ignorais qu'* (or *je ne savais pas qu'*) *il était marié*: 'I didn't know he was married.' But 'to ignore someone', in the sense of a social slight, might better be translated *faire semblant de ne pas voir (entendre, écouter) quelqu'un.*

Should you ever have occasion to style someone 'an ignoramus', *ignare* is the term you want.

illuminé (m). Loosely used to mean not only a visionary but also a demented person, *un fou*. So, it is definitely not the word that fits if you want to pay someone the compliment of calling him 'enlightened', which would be *éclairé*, or perhaps *évolué*. Similarly, *une lampe éclaire bien* ('a lamp gives good light'), or *une pièce est mal éclairée* ('a room is ill lit'), while *un monument est illuminé* ('a monument is floodlit'). *L'illumination*, 'floodlighting'.

impayable. Nothing to do with finances, but 'priceless' in the sense of 'too funny', 'the end', as said of an anecdote or of someone's expression in a snapshot.

important. An important, and rather tricky, adjective, for it means not only 'significant', but 'sizeable', 'impressive' as well. *Il importe de savoir lequel des deux rivaux a la fortune la plus importante* (v. IMPORTER). 'We must know which of the two rivals has the greater fortune.' *C'est l'immeuble le plus important qui ait été construit ici depuis vingt ans.* 'It is the biggest building that has been erected here in twenty years.'

importer. 'To import', first of all; and 'an importer', like 'an examiner', takes an extra syllable in French: *un importateur*.

'To be important', also—a verb which is lacking in English. *Il importe d'établir l'heure exacte à laquelle il est sorti.* 'The exact time at which he left is of vital importance.'

A most important derivation of this verb is the handful of *n'importe* expressions: *n'importe qui, n'importe quand, n'importe où, n'importe comment* . . . 'No matter who (anyone), no matter when (any time), no matter where (anywhere), no matter how (anyhow, any way).'

impression (f). You will do well to remember that this is the noun of two different verbs: *imprimer*, 'to print'; and *impressionner*, 'to impress' or 'to be impressive'. You may read of a book that it is the first *réimpression* of such and such a work in some years; and inside the book you may find *première impression, Janvier 1935; deuxième impression, Novembre 1935. Cet événement m'a grandement impressionné* (or *m'a fait une grande impression*). 'That event made a big impression on me.' 'Impressive' is expressed by the participle, *impressionnant*—which may be harder to remember than is *imposant* for 'imposing', since in the latter case both are participles.

incendie (m). First make a note of the surprising gender of a word that looks as though it should be feminine. *Un incendie* is bigger than *un feu*; you could not call *un feu de bois*, or *un feu de camp, un incendie. Un incendie* is what the firemen (*les [sapeurs-]pompiers*) are called out for.
   Faire du feu is 'to light a small fire', doing it deliberately, or 'to heat one's house'; *mettre le feu* is 'to set fire (to something) inadvertently'; while *incendier* is 'deliberately to set (something big) on fire'.

indicatif (m). The theme song or music habitually used to announce or conclude a program on the radio or on television.

indiquer. The verb to remember when you want to ask directions (*v.* DIRECTION). *Voulez-vous m'indiquer le chemin* (or *la route*) *pour aller à Chartres? Indication* (f) is the corresponding noun.
   Furthermore, 'to recommend'. On the bottle of *médicament* which you buy *chez le pharmacien*, you will read: *Indications: rhume, bronchite etc.* 'Recommended in cases of cold, bronchitis' etc. *Agir à son insu, ce n'est pas indiqué.* 'It is not advisable to act without his knowing of it.'
   Contre-indiquer, sometimes encountered in a medical context, is 'to advise against'. *Les cas de contre-indication de ce traitement sont les suivants.* 'This treatment is not recommended in the following cases.'

infect. Another of those adjectives which may surprise you. *Infect* has a wider meaning than *infecté* ('infected'), and is used in a more colloquial way. Students especially are likely to call the food in certain cheap restaurants *infect*: not 'infected', but simply 'filthy', 'lousy', 'incredibly bad', 'rotten'.

influer sur. An extra way, which may not occur to you at first, of saying *influencer* (transitive), or *avoir de l'influence sur quelqu'un*: 'to (have) influence (upon) someone'. *Une personne influente* is 'an influential person'.

innocenter. Like *importer* (q.v.), a verb lacking in English, and meaning 'to acquit', 'to clear someone'.

inscrire, s'. 'To register', or 'to matriculate', particularly in a school or university. *Les frais d'inscription* are 'tuition costs'. Also, in general, 'to sign up' as a member or supporter of something.

instantané. *Un instantané* is 'a snapshot'. 'Instant coffee', *Nescafé* (trade name), *café soluble*, or *café en poudre*.

intarissable. Said of someone who speaks neverendingly (on a particular subject). *Il (Elle) est intarissable.*

intéressé. With this adjective, we come upon a meaning which English has preserved mostly in the negative: 'disinterested', i.e. 'unselfish', or, 'not acting out of self-interest'. *Intéressé*, then, is 'self-interested' or, as one dictionary puts it, 'not disinterested'; and similarly, *intéressant* may be applied to something which is, or is likely to be, 'profitable' or 'advantageous'. As a noun, *l'intéressé(e)* is free of the pejorative air which may hang about the adjective, since it means simply 'the person involved *or* concerned'.

intérêt (m). Not only 'financial profit'—where it can be used in the plural (*On a rajouté les intérêts à mon livret de caisse d'épargne.* 'They've added the interest on to my savings account')—but any sort of 'advantage' or 'utility'. *Vous aurez intérêt à* (or *C'est dans votre intérêt de*) *lui laisser toute liberté de jeter sa gourme.* 'You will do well to let him sow his wild oats.' *Je ne vois pas l'intérêt* (*de faire cela*), 'I don't see the point (in doing that).'
    There is a nice distinction to be made. (*a*) *Ce livre n'est pas intéressant*: 'This is a dull book'. (*b*) *Ce livre est sans intérêt*: 'This book is worthless, of no value.' In the first instance, you stress the boring aspect of the book; in the second, the lack of profit derived from it.

interprète (m). Not only 'an interpreter', as in English, but often 'a singer', 'instrumentalist', 'actor', or other performing artist. The verb *interpréter* does not mean 'to interpret' as an interpreter does (*faire l'interprète*), but 'to comment', 'explain', 'sing', 'play', 'act', and so forth. *Cette chanson sera interprétée par* ... Or *l'interprète de cette sonate pour piano sera* ... 'This song will be sung by ...' Or 'this piano sonata will be played by ...' And of course, *l'interprétation* can mean 'rendition', 'singing', 'playing', 'acting'.

interroger, s'. Literally, 'to examine oneself'; 'to wonder', 'to engage in introspection', 'consider', 'reflect'. More formal than *se tâter*, which more clearly implies a hesitation between choices.

interrupteur (m). 'An electric light switch' (*v.* BRANCHER).

intoxication (f). One of the more memorable *Faux Amis*: it means 'poisoning' and not 'drunkenness', which is *l'ivresse* (f). If you want to sidestep the difficulty, you can say *empoisonnement* (m) for 'poisoning', but be forewarned that this last term also means 'a terrific nuisance', 'a bother'. *Quel empoisonnement!* 'What a nuisance!'

Il n'a que des empoisonnements (or *des tracas*) *à son bureau.* 'He's been having nothing but trouble at the office.'

invraisemblable. Since in English you rarely go around saying 'verisimilar', you may be surprised at the frequency with which *c'est invraisemblable* is used in French, meaning 'unlikely' or, more affirmatively, 'surprising', 'astonishing'. *C'était invraisemblable le nombre de gens venus l'écouter.* 'An astonishing number of people turned out to hear him.' *Vraisemblablement* is a quite acceptable substitute for *probablement*.

issue (f). First of all, this is not the word for an 'issue' of a magazine, newspaper etc. *Un numéro* is the right term.

L'issue is, however, 'the outlet' or 'exit' of a place or, in a more intangible situation, 'the way out', 'the solution'. *C'est sans issue* can be said as well of a dead-end road or cul-de-sac (*une voie sans issue*) as of an apparently hopeless or insoluble affair. The corresponding verb is *sortir*, *émerger* (*de la situation*), as there is no verb '*issuer*'. If you want to say that an odor 'issues' from somewhere, *se dégager de* or *émaner de* is the appropriate expression; *se faire entendre*, for a noise issuing from somewhere. *Des voix se firent entendre de derrière la porte.* 'The sound of voices issued from behind the door.'

J

Javel, eau de. Chlorine bleach for clothes. Scouring powders will sometimes be marked *javellisant*.

Javel is also a Métro stop in Paris. *L'Usine de Javel* is the Citroën works.

jeannette (f). 'The sleeve form' of an ironing board. 'The board' itself is *une planche à repasser* and 'the iron' is *le fer* (*à repasser*).

jet (m). A use not often stressed in a dictionary: 'the first draft' (of a manuscript, project and the like) is *le premier jet*.

Un jet d'eau, 'an (artificial) fountain'.

jeter. A reminder that paper handkerchiefs are given their functional name in French: *mouchoirs à jeter*; or sometimes, *mouchoirs en papier*. You buy them *chez le pharmacien* or *le marchand de couleurs*.

jeton (m). 'The token' which you need for telephoning from *une cabine publique*. Its price varies depending on whether you call from *la poste*—'the post office'—or from *un bureau de tabac*, 'a tobacconist's'. Calling from a *tabac* (q.v.) is more expensive, and nine times out of ten you buy your *jeton* at the counter before going downstairs to the phone booth *au sous-sol*.

jeunes, les (m. pl.). Frequently used in place of *la jeunesse*, to mean 'youth', 'the younger generation'. *Les jeunes de notre époque*, 'young people today'. Another of those *adjectifs substantivés*, like *le coupable* (q.v.).

Un terrain de jeu pour les jeunes is 'a playing field (*or* playground) for children or young people'.

Les vieux refers to 'old people', 'the older generation', and cannot, in this context, be replaced by *la vieillesse* (although you might expect an analogy with *la jeunesse*) but by *les vieillards*.

You might note that *les anciens* does not mean what *les vieux* means. *Les anciens* are 'the former members' of whatever it is : *une réunion des anciens du Lycée X*, 'a reunion (*or* meeting) of the former pupils of Lycée X'.

A common but not very courteous way of referring to one's parents is *mes vieux*, or *les vieux*.

jouer. A use which may not be made altogether clear in a dictionary : 'to act', 'to help' or 'influence'. *L'attitude de l'accusé a beaucoup joué en sa faveur*. 'The accused man's attitude greatly helped his case.'

juste. Surely you know that this means 'just', as opposed to 'unjust', *injuste*. But *juste* also means 'tight' (a dress), 'a near thing' (*J'ai eu mon train, mais c'était juste*), or 'barely sufficient' (*Il avait juste de quoi acheter le journal*); and sometimes, 'just' or 'only'. *Attendez-moi, je vais juste chercher mes affaires.* 'Wait for me, I'm just going to get my things.' 'A near thing' can also be expressed by *de justesse : nous sommes arrivés avant vous, mais de justesse.*

Justement!, like *précisément!*, signifies 'But that's just it!' 'That's just the point you were about to miss!'

Au juste, like a non-exclamatory *précisément*, means 'exactly'. *Mais j'y pense, quand est-ce qu'il part, au juste?* 'But come to think of it, just when is he leaving exactly?'

L

lacune (f). Rarely used in any but a figurative sense for 'a gap', 'a void'. *Il y a d'importantes lacunes dans ses connaissances géographiques.* 'His knowledge of geography is very spotty.' And the standard expression, *combler une lacune*, is 'to fill in the gap', 'supply the missing part', 'make up for a lack'.

The adjective 'spotty', 'faulty', is *lacuneux* or, *lacunaire*, but not commonly used.

langes (m. pl.). Not to be confused with *linge* (q.v.). *Des langes* are 'swaddling clothes', and the verb is *langer*, or *emmaillotter*.

larme (f). A neat way of protesting that you want only very little

—even less than *un doigt*—to drink: *Une larme seulement.* 'Just a drop please.'

lavabo (m). 'A washstand' or 'bathroom sink'. And very often, a euphemism for 'the lavatory'. *Où sont les lavabos?* (or *les toilettes* or *les cabinets*; or *les water*, pronounced waterre; or *les W.C.* or *V.C.*, pronounced as the letters are pronounced in the French alphabet). In a café, 'the lavatory' will most often be called *les toilettes* and be *au fond de la salle*—'in the back of the room'—or *au sous-sol*, 'downstairs'. In either case, it will be next to the telephone booth.

lèche-vitrines (m). 'Window-shopping'. *Le samedi matin elles aiment faire du lèche-vitrines.* 'They like to go window-shopping on Saturday morning'.

liaison (f). The word for '(love) affair'. *Une affaire* will never do here. Cf: Laclos, *Les Liaisons Dangereuses*.

'To be in touch with someone' is *être en liaison avec quelqu'un* or, less militarily, *être en contact avec quelqu'un*.

You might note that it is possible to overdo the sort of liaison which you have been taught to do in speaking, as in *allez-y*. Une fausse liaison like '*c'est mal-t'à-propos*', or '*c'est d'un joli zeffet*' is quite illegitimate, although it may seem to be called for, particularly when two vowels occur together. This sort of error may come naturally and is quite forgivable, but it is really good only for laughs.

licencié. If you are *licencié*, either you have *une licence* (roughly, an M.A.), or you have been laid off, given the sack (*un licenciement*). *Toucher une forte indemnité de licenciement* is 'to get a large amount of severance pay'. If you resign, *vous démissionnez*, or *vous donnez votre démission*, *la démission* being 'resignation'. This necessitates 'giving a month's notice': *donner un mois de préavis*. For another use of *préavis*, *v.* the chapter on LE TÉLÉPHONE.

In either case, *licencié* is not to be confused with *licencieux*, which means 'licentious'.

'To be licensed to' do or to sell something, *avoir une patente*.

ligne (f). *Les grandes lignes* indicates 'the outline', or 'the main points', of a situation or project. *Le patron n'a fait que donner les grandes lignes du nouveau projet, sans entrer dans les détails.* 'The boss only outlined the new plan, without going into detail.'

At the railway station, however, *les grandes lignes* refers to 'the interurban trains', as opposed to *les trains de banlieue*, 'suburban trains'.

limonade (f). If on a hot, dry afternoon you order this at a *terrasse*, you may be disappointed when the *garçon* brings you, not 'lemonade', but 'lemon-flavored soda water' (*eau pétillante*). What you probably meant was *un citron pressé*: lemon juice, sugar, and ordinary water (*eau plate*). Nor has *limonade* anything to do with limes (*citron vert*), which you will be very lucky to find, ever, at any French *terrasse*.

linge (m). Clean linen, personal and household; also, dirty linen, the washing, particularly when given out as laundry. The *blanchisserie* will often mark *linge au poids*, meaning washing done at so much per kg. and not per item.

La lingerie, you will remember, is not only women's underclothing (which is more properly *la lingerie fine*) but the linen trade as well, or even a linen room or closet.

La lessive is generally the washing you do yourself—*faire sa lessive*—as opposed to *donner son linge à laver*; and *la lessive* can also be the soapflakes or powder used in washing. *La lessiveuse*, 'washtub'. *Machine à laver*, washing machine.

Être lessivé is a definitely *familier* way of saying 'to be worn out *or* dog-tired'.

M

machin (m). A verbal crutch, corresponding to 'thingumabob', 'whatd'yacallit', 'what'shisname'. You can overdo it, of course, and even compound it by saying *machin-chose* (m), but often you'll find there's no getting around it. Definitely spoken, not written, French; an even more colloquial form is *bidule* (m) (*v.* also TRUC).

magnétophone (m). 'A tape recorder'. 'The tape' is *la bande magnétique*; 'to tape record' is *enregistrer sur bande magnétique*; 'tape recording' is *un enregistrement sur bande magnétique*. 'To erase', *effacer*.

maigre. 'Thin', 'meager'. In speaking of a person, it is more tactful to say *mince*, or even *svelte*.

When it comes to cheese and yogurt, it denotes a low fat content (*v.* GRAISSE).

Not to be confused with *écrémé*: literally 'decreamed', i.e. 'skimmed'.

maison (f). 'House' or 'home', of course. But you will often hear 'le home', which today's Frenchman seems to feel more adequate than *la maison* or *le foyer* to express the idea of intimacy which attaches to the English 'home'. 'To go home': *rentrer à la maison, rentrer chez soi*.

Also, 'house', in the sense of 'a business firm'. But it will never do for a doctor's, dentist's, or barrister's (lawyer's) office, which is *un cabinet*; nor for a *notaire*'s, which is *une étude*. (When telephoning for an appointment or for information, you ask: *C'est le cabinet du Dr. Untel? C'est l'étude de Maître Machin?*) Nor for a hairdresser's, which is *un salon de coiffure*. In the case of any small one-man practice or business, the best thing to do when telephoning is to use the person's name only.

mal (m., or adv.). As in the case of *bien, bon,* and *mauvais,* one could go on for paragraphs of idiomatic expressions and clichés. Let us confine ourselves to the following items, few but basic:

Pas mal! or *Pas si mal (que ça)!* Quite the equivalent of 'not bad'; in other words, 'pretty good'. A common understated form of praise or appreciation. As in the English expression, the intonation is important.

Elle n'est pas mal du tout: 'She's quite pretty' (*v.* PAS MAL).

Il ne s'en est pas tiré si mal que ça, or more colloquially: *Il s'en est pas mal tiré.* 'He got out of it (*or* over it) pretty nicely.'

Il n'y a pas de mal is the polite response to someone's apology for having, let us say, stepped on your foot or wakened you by telephoning too early in the morning.

Avoir mal is 'to be in pain'; *avoir du mal (à faire quelque chose)* is 'to have trouble (doing something)'. *Se donner du mal,* 'to go to a lot of trouble'. *Faire mal,* 'to hurt (physically)'; *faire du mal,* 'to harm' (in the abstract). *Ça lui fait mal quand il marche,* 'it hurts him when he walks'. *Ça lui fait du mal de marcher.* 'Walking doesn't do him any good.' Beware of *mal au cœur,* which has nothing to do with 'heartache', being simple 'nausea'. *Mal au ventre* is ordinary 'stomach ache'.

malicieux. May be a *Faux Ami,* as it means 'mischievous'; *la malice* is 'mischief'.

For 'malicious' and 'malice', use *méchant* and *la méchanceté.*

manchette (f). 'Cuff'; 'a cuff link' is *un bouton de manchette.*

Also, 'a big headline' in the newspaper; the general term for headline is *un titre.*

mannequin (m). 'A fashion model', if it's a living person, or else 'a dummy'. But be careful how you translate 'model' in any other context. 'A model train', for instance, is not *un mannequin* but *un train miniature.* 'A scale model' of an architectural project is *une maquette* (*q.v.*). A 'model child' is, however, *un enfant modèle.*

manquer. You know that *manquer* means, roughly, 'to miss'—someone, a train, doing something, one's aim, and so on. You have certainly been warned a dozen times that 'I miss you' turns out in French 'you miss me' ('you are missing to me'). But even experienced speakers *ne manquent pas de tomber dans les nombreux pièges tendus par le verbe 'manquer'.* So let us just run through a handful of examples:

Elle m'a manqué. 'I missed her.'

Je lui ai manqué. 'She (he) missed me.'

J'ai manqué mon bus. 'I missed the bus.'

J'ai manqué de (j'ai failli) me faire écraser. 'I nearly got run over.'

Il manque quatre pages à la fin du Tome Premier. 'Four pages are missing from the end of Volume I.'

Il manque de respect. 'He is lacking in respect (is disrespectful).'

C'est un manque (de tact etc.). 'It's a lack (of tact), a defect *or* weakness'.

Bien des choses à votre mère.—Je n'y manquerai pas. 'Give my regards to your mother.' 'I certainly shall.'

Il ne manquerait plus que ça! 'That would be the last straw!'

Un manque à gagner, 'a profit missed'.

Manquer is sometimes used interchangeably with *rater* or *louper*, as in the example with the bus, above. *J'ai manqué (loupé, raté) mon dessin*. 'My drawing did not come out.' *Il s'est manqué*. 'His suicide attempt failed.'

maquette (f). 'A scale model' of a car, a building, a statue, and the like. The person who makes it is *le maquettiste*. Not to be confused with *la moquette*, 'wall-to-wall carpeting' (*v.* also MANNEQUIN).

marché (m). 'The market'; *un marché découvert*, 'an open-air market'. *Faire le marché*, 'to go marketing'. When you do, you will find *un filet*, 'a net *or* string shopping-bag', indispensable.

Fruit and vegetables are sold mostly *au poids* ('according to weight') and more specifically, *au kilo(gramme)*, 'so much per kilogram'. Occasionally they are sold at so much apiece, as with melons (e.g. *2 F pièce*); or 'per bunch', *la botte (de radis*, for example); or even *le tas*, 'the pile', of two or three heads of lettuce. 'A bunch of celery' is not *une botte* but *un pied de céleri*. 'A whole garlic' is *une tête d'ail*, and each of its cloves is *une gousse*. *Un marchand des quatre saisons* is 'an itinerant vendor', with a wagon instead of a stall.

Marchander is 'to bargain' to bring down the price; something which it is better not to try in the ordinary *marché* in town.

marcher. One of the words the English-speaking resident in France is likely to pick up most quickly and to delight most in using, in a sort of Frenchified English, *pour rire* ('just for laughs').

You might start by refreshing your memory as to what the word does not generally mean. It does not often mean 'to march', which is more properly *défiler* or *marcher au pas*. Nor does it mean 'to market', which is *vendre, mettre en vente*; 'to do the marketing' is *faire le marché, faire ses courses, aller au marché*.

It is a way of saying 'to walk', like *aller à pied* or *faire (le trajet) à pied*. It is above all a way of saying 'to run'—as a car; 'to function', 'to work' or 'succeed'—as any plan or scheme; or, in any of these senses, 'to go'. *La marche* is 'walking', or 'walk'. *Le prochain village est à trois heures de marche d'ici.* 'The next village is three hours' walk from here.' *La marche à pied est le meilleur exercice.* 'Walking is the best exercise.' *Les chaussures de marche,* 'walking shoes'. *Ma voiture marche mal.* 'My car doesn't run very well.' *Il croyait avoir des places gratuites, mais ça n'a pas marché.* 'He thought he'd have free seats, but it didn't work.'

More slangily, *marcher* means 'to fall for something', 'to be taken in'; and *faire marcher quelqu'un,* 'to fool someone', 'make a sucker of him'. *Il a marché comme un seul homme.* 'He swallowed it, hook, line and sinker.' *La marche arrière* is 'reverse gear' in a car; 'to back up' or 'go into reverse' is *reculer, se mettre en marche arrière, faire marche arrière.*

Une marche (or less commonly, *un degré*) is a step of a flight of stairs.

marier. Lest you forget, you have a transitive and a reflexive intransitive form, and they do not mean the same thing. *Marier quelqu'un* is 'to marry *or* pair someone off to someone else'; whereas *se marier avec quelqu'un* is the equivalent of a different, transitive verb, *épouser quelqu'un:* 'to marry someone'. *Un mariage* is both 'wedding' and 'marriage'. If you want to stress the ceremonial, or wedding, aspect, you have to say *la cérémonie (nuptiale)* or *les noces. La mariée* is of course 'the bride'; 'the groom' is *le marié.*

You can say that a mixture or a blend of two colors, two sorts of humor and so forth is *un mariage réussi.*

Epouser can also mean 'to adhere strictly' (to an idea), or 'to fit tightly'; so conceivably you could say of a dress *qu'elle épouse les hanches et qu'elle est un heureux mariage de vert et de bleu!*

maroquinerie (f). The normal term for 'a leather-goods shop'— gloves, handbags, luggage. You may sometimes see it styled *une sellerie,* but this is an affectation, since you're not likely nowadays to find any saddles sold there. *Une bourrellerie,* however, if you can locate one, is still likely to live up to its name and sell not only harness but all sorts of leather straps.

marque (f). Among other things, 'brand-name', 'trade-mark' or 'make'. 'A mark' or 'grade', in the scholastic sense, is *une note.*

méridional. 'Southern', as *un accent méridional,* 'an accent of the south of France'. *Un méridional* is 'a southerner', 'a person from the Midi'. The contrary, *septentrional,* meaning 'northern', is used only for regions. 'A northerner' is *une personne du nord.*

mètre (m). Just to remind you that the metric system obtains in France. Distance is counted in *kilomètres,* abbreviated *km,* roughly 3/5 of a mile. In buying *de l'essence* ('petrol'; US: 'gasoline') for your car, you calculate how many *litres* you use *au cent,* 'per hundred kilometers'. Rooms are measured in *mètres carrés,* 'square meters', abbreviated m^2. People too are measured in meters: *mon frère est assez grand, il mesure un* *mètre 83 (centimètres).* 'My brother is quite tall, about six feet.' 'A tape measure' is *un mètre à ruban* (or a *décamètre*, as the case may be). *Un mètre* may also be 'a ruler' one meter long, although a shorter or a longer ruler is *une règle.*

mettre. One of those protean verbs that can mean any number of things, in addition to the 'to put' and 'to place' that your grammar book certainly mentions.

For instance, 'what shall I wear' (i.e. 'put on') is simply *qu'est-ce que je vais (me) mettre?*, although 'to wear' the clothes, once you've put them on, is *porter.*

Se mettre à faire quelque chose is often a convenient substitute for *commencer: il s'est mis à bailler*, 'he began to yawn'. *S'y mettre* is, more specifically, 'to set about doing a given task', 'to buckle down to work'.

Mettre en état—'to restore' something, to get it into good or working condition—is only one of a handful of expressions with *mettre en: en marche, en cause, en scène, en page, en ordre, en musique*; and as you can see, here *mettre* must be translated in as many different ways: 'to start', 'to implicate', 'to direct (a play)', 'to lay out', 'to arrange' or 'put in order', 'to set to music'.

In sports jargon, *mettre la gomme* is 'to step up speed'.

mettre en valeur. A phrase greatly in fashion these days, as applied to the development or improvement of a hitherto undeveloped or rundown neighborhood or region, usually with the idea of attracting tourist trade or business. *Actuellement on parle beaucoup de mettre en valeur la Camargue.* 'There is much talk these days of developing the Camargue area.' The noun is *la mise en valeur.*

In other circumstances, *mettre quelque chose en valeur* is simply 'to set off or enhance something'. *Le vert de sa robe met en valeur ses yeux.* 'The green of her dress sets off her eyes.'

mielleux. May prove something of a *Faux Ami*, since it does not mean 'having a taste of honey', which is usually *ayant un goût de miel. Mielleux* is used figuratively, like 'honeyed' in English, to mean 'flattering', 'hypocritical'. *Des paroles mielleuses*, 'honeyed words'.

moins. It might be useful to clarify a use of *à moins: Elle a eu si peu de veine qu'elle est très déprimée. On le serait à moins!* 'She's been so unlucky that she's very much depressed. Who wouldn't be?' In other words, used in this way, with a conditional tense and most often with *on, à moins* means 'who can blame him?' or 'it doesn't take that much to be' (or 'do', or whatever the context calls for).

moisir. 'To rot' or 'grow moldy'; and by extension, in speaking of a person, 'to stay somewhere too long'. *Ne moisissez pas dans* *cette place, vous y perdriez votre temps.* 'Don't hang on to that job too long; it's a waste of time.'

monde (m). If you examine the expression *tout le monde*, you realize that *monde* here means neither 'earth' nor even 'world' in a political sense, but a given 'population' or 'society'. So that to say *nous avons du monde ce soir*, 'we have some people coming over this evening', follows naturally. Similarly, *il y avait un monde fou au bal*, 'there was a terrific crowd at the dance'. And *s'il y a trop de monde chez le boucher, ce n'est pas la peine d'attendre*—'if there's too long a queue at the butcher's, don't bother to wait'.

Used in another sort of phrase altogether, *un monde* can mean 'a big fuss': *l'incident est sans importance, mais il en fait tout un monde.* 'What happened is insignificant, but he's making a mountain out of a molehill.'

The adjective 'worldly' is *mondain*; 'a worldly person', *un(e) mondain(e)*, or less ambiguously, *un homme (une femme) de monde. La brigade mondaine* designates policemen assigned to moral offences, drugs, etc.

monnaie (f). A classic *Faux Ami*, as you undoubtedly know, but a slip of the tongue comes when you least expect it. *La monnaie* is 'change', 'small change', 'coins'; *l'argent* is 'money'. *Faire la monnaie d'un billet de 100*, 'to turn a 100 franc note into change'.

If you want to say of someone that he is 'monied', *monnayé* will not do; *riche, fortuné*, or *à son aise* is what you need. *Monnayer* means merely 'to make money out of something' (an object, a title, etc.), 'to trade something for money', but not in the sense of pawning it (*v.* MONT-DE-PIÉTÉ).

mont-de-piété (m). 'The pawnshop' now called *Crédit Municipal*. The old-fashioned individual 'pawnbroker' is *le prêteur sur gages. J'ai mis* (or *engagé*) *ma montre au mont-de-piété.* 'I've pawned my watch.'

(In terms far more *familier*, you say *J'ai mis ma montre au clou*, or *chez ma tante.*)

Never ever confuse *mont-de-piété* and *articles* (or *objets*) *de piété!*, the latter being 'devotional objects'.

moudre. 'To grind.' One of those infinitives you rarely need but when you buy ground coffee, you need to know the past participle, *moulu.* (Nothing to do with *mouler*, 'to mold', whose past participle is perfectly regular: *moulé.*) *Un moulin à café* is 'a coffee grinder'; while *une moule* is 'a mussel' and *un moule* 'a mold'.

mouvement d'humeur (m). 'A fit of bad temper', 'an ill-tempered gesture'. An expression worth noting because (1) it is quite frequent, (2) the sort of *humeur* implied is always *la mauvaise*, and (3) this is as good a place as any to recall that *l'humeur* (f) is not *l'humour* (m). The first is generally 'mood', as in *être de bonne humeur*, 'to be in a good mood'. *L'humour* is clear enough; *avoir de l'humour* is 'to have a (good) sense of humor'. The adjective 'humorous' is *humoristique*, with a troublesome change in spelling.

moyennant. A preposition which may often be found in place of *contre*: 'against' or 'in exchange for' (a sum of money, a promise, or whatever).

N

nager. 'To swim'. *Se baigner*, 'to bathe', is not quite the same. *Baigner quelqu'un* or, more commonly, *donner un bain à quelqu'un*, is 'to bathe someone else'.

    The art of swimming is *la natation*, but the act itself is *la nage*. *Traverser la Manche à la nage*, 'to swim across the Channel'. Neither one, however, will do for 'a swimming pool', which is *une piscine*, nor for 'a swimsuit', which is *un maillot* (or *un costume*) *de bain*.

    In conversation you may hear *je nage*, meaning 'I'm lost', 'I don't get it', 'I don't follow'. But someone *qui sait nager* is someone who can stay afloat in business, who knows how to get along.

navet (m). 'The turnip', of course; but often used exactly as 'dud' is used in English to express 'a flop'—as a film or other performance—or worthless work of art.

n'est-ce pas? In English, you are so allergic to the double negative that a sentence like *Il n'est pas parti, n'est-ce pas?* ('He didn't go, did he?') may strike your ear as a flagrant error, whereas it is as perfectly correct as *Il est parti, n'est-ce pas?* ('He did go, didn't he?'). The matter of 'question tags'—'have you?', 'shouldn't they?', 'aren't I?', and so forth—so troublesome to foreigners learning English, is simplicity itself in French. You can even add *n'est-ce pas?* to a phrase which at first glance appears a double or triple negative all by itself, like *aucun billet n'est plus valable.* 'All tickets are invalid.'

    N'est-ce pas? is also a matter of personal style in conversation; many speakers will interrupt their own train of thought with it by way of affirmation, just as you might say 'don't you see?' or 'right?'

non plus. Often used by itself, and in repetition to express a series of 'neither', 'no more do I', and the like.—*Avez-vous vu votre oncle?* —*Non.* —*Votre tante?* —*Non plus.* —*Votre cousine alors?* —*Non plus.*

O

obligatoire. 'Compulsory.' Used much more often than you would say 'obligatory' in English. *Obligatoirement*, like *forcément* and *nécessairement*, means 'necessarily', 'compulsorily'.

In terms of the highway code, *un sens obligatoire* is the opposite of *un sens interdit*; that is, 'a one-way street' or road which you have to take, as opposed to 'a no-entry' or 'a one-way' in the 'wrong' way.

occasion (f). First of all, 'a chance'. *J'ai eu l'occasion de le rencontrer.* 'I had a chance to meet him' (*v.* CHANCE). *Par la même occasion*, 'at the same time', 'while one is at it'.

And sometimes, 'a lucky chance' or 'find'. *J'ai vu une de ces robes! Alors, j'ai sauté sur l'occasion!* 'I saw such a marvellous dress! I jumped at the chance.'

Acheter d'occasion is 'to buy secondhand'.

occuper. *Etre occupé*, 'to be busy'; can be said as well of a person as of a telephone line. *La ligne est occupée.*

S'occuper de is one of those expressions which may not occur to you on the first try, since it differs so much from the English 'to take care of', 'to look after (something)'. *Je vais m'en occuper.* 'I'll take care of it.' In a shop, an attentive salesman will ask: *Monsieur, on s'occupe de vous?* 'May I help you, sir?'—literally, 'is someone (else) already taking care of you?'

œuf (f). 'An egg'; you pronounce the *f*, as in *bœuf*. But the plural, *œufs*, works like the plural *bœufs*; the *f* is forgotten, so that *œufs* is pronounced like the pronoun *eux*.

Un œuf brouillé: 'scrambled egg'
— *à la coque*: 'soft-boiled'
— *mollet*: 'medium-boiled'
— *dur*: 'hard-boiled'
— *poché*: 'poached'
— *sur le plat*: 'fried'
Une omelette: 'omelette'
Le jaune, 'yolk'. *Le blanc*, 'white'.

L'épicier will often mark the eggs he sells *œufs coque*, meaning 'extra-fresh eggs', for soft-boiling.

on. You are aware of the grammatical properties of the impersonal pronoun, and of the fact that it is most often translated by the passive voice. *On lui a dit de le faire.* 'He was told to do it.' But a good deal less stigma attaches to constructions with *on* than to the use of the passive in English. A word of caution, however: it is very easy to let *on* run away with you and to use it as a lazy way out of remembering the verb forms that go with more accurate pronouns. For instance: *On ne savait plus quoi faire, alors on est allé au cinéma.* Whereas you mean *Nous ne savions plus quoi faire, alors nous sommes allés au cinéma.*

oui. Even if you have an otherwise flawless accent, your French is not totally authentic until you have learned to deal with *oui.* As it is so often uttered, it is more of a gasp than anything else, a soft sharp *ssshing* intake of breath, neither *'voui'* nor *'ouish'* but somewhere in between.

P

pain (m). One of the most celebrated things about France. When you go to buy it at *la boulangerie* or in certain *pâtisseries*, you'll need to indicate whether you want *une baguette*, for instance, or *une ficelle, un bâtard, un saucisson, une couronne, une petite* (or *une grosse) boule*, depending on the shape and the size; *un pain de campagne, un pain de seigle, un pain brioché, un pain moulé, fariné, bien cuit, pas trop cuit,* and so on.

Le pain grillé is 'toast'; *un grille-pain*, 'a toaster'.

You should be aware that *avoir du pain sur la planche* is a much-used way of saying 'to have a lot of work lined up', 'to have a lot to do'.

Un pain can also be 'a cake' (*de savon*) or 'a lump' or 'loaf' (*de sucre*). *Avoir quelque chose pour une bouchée de pain* means 'to buy it for a song, for next to nothing'.

pan pan pan! 'Bang bang!'

pantalon (m). 'A pair of trousers *or* pants' is called simply *un pantalon*; and 'a pair of shorts', *un short.*

papier (m). The first thing to commit to memory here is that *le papier* can refer to any sort of paper but the newspaper, which is *le journal.*

Papier à lettres par avion, 'air-mail paper'
— *de brouillon*, 'scrap (first draft) paper'
— *carbone*, 'carbon paper'
— *pour doubles*, 'onion skin'
— *d'emballage*, 'brown wrapping paper'
— *à en-tête de la maison*, 'letterhead stationery'
— *hygiénique*, 'toilet paper'
— *pour machine à écrire*, 'typing paper'
— *de soie*, 'tissue paper'
— *timbré*, 'official stamped paper' (for documents)

papillon (m). 'Butterfly' or 'moth'; any small detachable slip of paper; and most especially, the pet name for the notice which the *agent de police* sticks on the windshield of your car to inform you that you've been fined for illegal parking. *Un* *nœud papillon* is a man's 'bow tie', as opposed to *une cravate*, an ordinary 'straight tie'.

parages (m. pl.). Used in *dans les parages.* 'in the neighborhood', 'near here'. *Je l'ai vu passer tout à l'heure, il doit être toujours dans les parages.* 'I saw him go by just a minute ago; he must still be somewhere around here.'

parc (m). One way of saying 'park', although *le bois, le jardin, le square* may occur as frequently: *le Bois de Boulogne, le jardin des Tuileries. Amener un enfant au square,* 'to take a child out to the (small) park'. 'A square', as in 'Trafalgar Square', is translated by *une place.*

Un parc may also be 'a baby's playpen'.

'A car-park' is *un parking.* There is a curious expression which you may think means 'a car-park' but which means in fact the total number of cars in France: *le parc automobile.*

parent (m). Both a *Vrai* and a *Faux Ami. Un parent* is indeed 'a parent'—but also any other relative. The word *relations* (q.v.) does exist and is even a very vital part of your vocabulary, but it has nothing to do with 'relatives'.

You must use caution in approaching all relatives beginning with *beau-* and *belle-*, since these prefixes are used both for 'step-' and for '-in-law'. *Un beau-père* is your 'father-in-law', or your 'stepfather'; *belle-mère* works the same way. So do *beau-frère* and *belle-sœur, beau-fils* and *belle-fille,* although in these last two cases you can get around the difficulty by using *gendre* (m) and *bru* (f), respectively, when you mean the -in-law sort. *La bru* is used less and less nowadays, however; and *marâtre,* the alternative for 'stepmother', still less. Today, *marâtre* has come to mean 'a bad *or* wicked mother', *une mère indigne.*

part (f). *De la part de* is a very vital little phrase: 'from So-and-So', 'on behalf of So-and-So', 'with the recommendation of So-and-So'. *Je vous écris de la part de M. Untel,* when you write to request a favor, helps your cause immeasurably: 'I come to you recommended by Mr. So-and-So.' *Il m'a remis ce mot de la part de sa tante.* 'He gave me this note on behalf of his aunt.' *Dites-lui de ma part . . .* 'Tell him from me . . .' When it comes to cakes, and to certain cheeses, *une part* is 'a portion'.

partance (f). 'The departure' of a boat, train, or plane. At the *gare de chemin de fer* there is generally a special set of *guichets* ('windows') marked *En Partance,* for those who have to buy their tickets in a hurry because their train is to pull out in a few minutes.

particulier. 'Private.' *Un particulier,* 'a private individual'. *Une maison particulière,* 'a private house'.

partition (f). 'A musical score.' 'A partition (wall)' is *une cloison.*

pas mal. 'Not bad!', or 'a fair number' etc. *Il y avait pas mal de monde.* 'There were quite a lot of people' (*v.* MAL).

passer. A verb with manifold uses. Without trying to go into all of them, you might recall that:

passer un examen does not mean 'to succeed in an exam' but merely 'to sit for (take) it';

passons, like *glissons*, can be very fatalistic: *Il ne m'a jamais rendu l'argent que je lui ai prêté, mais enfin, passons.* 'He's never paid back the money I lent him, but let's not talk about it any more' *or*, 'never mind';

passer une visite médicale is 'to go through a medical examination';

passer quelque chose à quelqu'un is either 'to hand *or* lend someone something', or 'to forgive someone something': *Il l'aime à la folie et lui passe tous ses caprices.* 'He's mad about her and puts up with all her whims.'

se passer de quelque chose is 'to do without something';

. . . *et j'en passe et des meilleurs*, very colloquial, means, 'I know a lot more about it but I'll spare you the details', or, 'not to mention . . .'; and *passer chez quelqu'un* or *passer voir quelqu'un* is the nearest thing to 'to drop in on someone'.

passible. The adjective which expresses one type of 'liable': the legal sort, meaning 'punishable by', 'subject to'. *Toute personne jetant des papiers sur la voie ferrée sera passible d'une amende.* 'Anyone who throws papers on the railway tracks is liable to a fine.'

But the 'liable' which expresses unwelcome likelihood requires different treatment altogether. 'The boss is liable to come and criticize your work'. *Il y a de fortes chances pour que le patron vienne critiquer votre travail*, or *Il est probable que le patron vienne* . . .

'Not likely!' can be handled in several ways: *Ça m'étonnerait! Vous n'y pensez pas! Invraisemblable!* —among others.

passif (m). 'The passive voice'; also 'debits'. *Avoir quelque chose à son passif* is 'to have something—in one's activities or one's past record—which is on the debit side', as *un séjour en prison*. *Avoir quelque chose à son actif*, 'to have something to one's credit.' *Ce jeune metteur en scène a déjà trois pièces à son actif.* 'This young director has already done three plays, *or*, has three plays to his credit'.

pâté maison (m). An item which may—and should—appear on the menu: a *pâté* made by, or in the style of, the restaurant itself. Not to be confused with *le pâté de maisons*, 'the block of houses'! *Je vais juste faire le tour du pâté de maisons.* 'I'm just going for a walk around the block.'

Une pâtée is 'cat *or* dog food'.

patron (m). Corresponds quite accurately to 'boss', which means that it is widely used and also very casual. So if you are being interviewed or summoned by your superior on a white-collar job, you don't call him *Patron* but *Monsieur le Directeur*.

Un patron being the 'pattern' used in sewing, it is also a way of indicating average or medium size in certain types of men's clothing, especially pajamas and underclothes; you have *demi-patron, patron*, and *grand patron*.

pattemouille (f.). The dampened cloth you put over clothes you want to steam iron.

pavés (m. pl.). 'The paving blocks *or* stones' making up *la chaussée*, the surface of the road. If you mean 'pavement', in British English (or 'sidewalk', in American English), then you say *le trottoir*.

pays (m.). You may have trouble getting used to the idea that *un pays* is just as often a small region or even a town as it is a nation or country. *C'est un petit pays, mais bien joli.* 'The region is small, but quite pretty.' *Il y a un poste d'essence à la sortie du pays.* 'There's a petrol (gas) station at the edge of town.' *Il est le seul médecin de tout le pays.* 'He's the only doctor in all the country round', 'in these parts'.

Less often, *un pays* can even be a local fellow, a native of one's small home town; *une payse* is the feminine equivalent.

peine (f.). Some very useful expressions you should know how to wield readily:

se donner la peine de, 'to go to the trouble of (doing something)'. *Je vous remercie de toute la peine* (or *de tout le mal*) *que vous vous êtes donné(es)*. 'Thank you for going to so much trouble.' *Ne vous donnez pas la peine, je vous prie.* 'Please don't bother.' A much less formal version of which is *non merci, ce n'est pas la peine. Cela ne vaut pas la peine* (*ce n'est pas la peine*) can be used quite differently, indicating 'there's no point in doing that', 'it's no use'. *Ce n'est pas la peine de le gronder, il ne travaillera pas pour autant.* 'It's no use scolding him; it won't make him work.' *Faire de la peine à quelqu'un*, 'to hurt *or* disappoint someone'. *Une situation pénible* is 'an embarrassing *or* morally difficult situation'. (If you mean 'physical pain', then you need to say *la douleur*, and *douloureux*.) *Il est pénible, ce garçon!* 'What a boring (*or* hardly bearable) fellow he is!'

pencher, se. A common expression with a rather striking image is *se pencher sur la question*: literally, 'to lean over the matter at hand'. Said most often of *les experts, les savants. Depuis des années, les médecins se penchent sur le problème du cancer.* 'For years doctors have been making a close study of cancer.'

pense-bête (m.). A reminder to do something, such as a string tied around your finger or a knot in your handkerchief.

penser. We want to call your attention to the nuances of *penser* with *bien. Les gens bien pensants* are 'right-thinking people', an expression sometimes used with irony, becoming downright pejorative.

Penser bien (or *bien penser*) is a frequent, more emphatic form of the verb, as may be the case with *sembler* and *croire*. *J'ai bien pensé* (or *il m'a bien semblé*) *qu'il était gêné*. 'I had the distinct impression that he was embarrassed.' *Mais je pense bien!* means 'I should think so!' or 'but definitely!'

And as you surely know, whereas the Englishman will say 'I think so', the Frenchman more readily 'believes so': *je crois que oui*—or, if he is contradicting something you've said in the negative—*je crois que si*. 'I don't think so', *je crois que non*, *je ne crois pas*.

permettre. *Vous permettez?* is the most common, and indispensable, formula for 'may I?' when, for instance, you want to share a seat with someone on the bus or reach for the salt. You may also hear *puis-je?*, but this is a good deal more casual and so is not to be used unless you know at least the name of the person, of an equal status with yourself.

Pérou (m). The South American country, yes; but far more importantly, 'Eldorado', 'riches', and always used in the negative: *ce n'est pas le Pérou*. 'It's nothing to get excited about; it's no fortune.'

personne (f). 'A person' of either sex. This word provides you with a readymade means to discretion when the occasion calls for it; *une personne a téléphoné* can mean that either a man or a woman has telephoned. But you must be careful; when you use *personne* in the negative—*je n'ai vu personne*—it becomes a masculine pronoun, although for all practical purposes it is still asexual. *Personne n'a téléphoné, personne n'est venu.* 'Nobody called, nobody came.' *Personne n'est parfait.* 'No one is perfect'. You hear *les grandes personnes* far more often than *les adultes*, to mean 'grown-ups' or 'adults'.

petit(e) ami(e). 'Boy *or* girl friend', as the case may be, or 'sweet-heart', if you prefer an old-fashioned term.

petitesse (f). 'Smallness' in physical terms or, more often and like *mesquinerie* (f), a 'moral smallness *or* meanness'.

petit-fils (m). Just a reminder that this does not usually mean 'little son' but 'grandson'. One's 'little boy' is one's *petit garçon*, or simply one's *fils*. The confusion may be greater with *petite fille*, which means not only 'granddaughter' (written *petite-fille*) but also 'little girl' or 'very young daughter' (your own or anyone else's). A great-grandson obviously cannot be '*un grand petit-fils*'. You say *un arrière-petit-fils*. Similarly, for 'great-granddaughter' as well as 'great-grandfather' and 'great-grandmother'—*arrière-petite-fille, arrière-grand-père, arrière grand'mère*. But 'a great-aunt *or* -uncle' is *grand-tante* or *grand-oncle*, and *arrière* enters into the picture in this case only when you need to express 'great-great-uncle (-aunt)', *arrière-grand-oncle (-tante)*.

pied (m). 'Foot', of course; and if you want to say how tall you are without stopping to figure it out in centimeters, you say *5 pieds 11 pouces*, '5 feet 11 inches'.

Pied is found in so many idioms and set phrases that you may lose your own footing at first. Look for instance at (*a*) *Faire des pieds et des mains (pour avoir quelque chose)*; (*b*) *Faire les pieds à quelqu'un*; and (*c*) *Se faire la main*. The first is 'to move heaven and earth (to obtain something)'. The second, rather *familier*, is 'to give someone his just desserts': *Tu n'as qu'à partir sans lui; ça lui fera les pieds!* 'Why don't you just leave without him; that'll serve him right!' The third, quite proper, is 'to get one's hand in', 'do a bit of apprenticeship', 'get used to something new'.

Faire un pied de nez is 'to cock a snook' or 'thumb one's nose', whereas *faire le pied de grue* is 'to be made to wait for someone', 'to dance attendance'.

'To take something literally' is *prendre quelque chose au pied de la lettre*. And 'to blunder' is *mettre les pieds dans le plat*, an expression which is definitely more *familier* than *faire une gaffe*.

Travailler d'arrache-pied is by no means to be confused with *travailler comme un pied* (or *comme un sabot*), the first meaning 'to work very hard' and the second, 'to work badly', 'to botch one's work'. And finally you have *partir les pieds devant*, 'to kick the bucket'.

pile (f). Any sort of 'electric battery'; but the battery of a car is called *la batterie*, as is the complete range of kitchen utensils, including *les casseroles*, *le tamis*, *le batteur à œufs*, *les passoires*, *les râpes*, *les poêles*, and so forth.

La batterie also means, especially when it comes to jazz bands, all of the drums and percussion instruments.

'A pile' of something is, generally speaking, *un tas*.

Pile ou face, 'heads or tails'.

piston (m). 'A valuable connection', 'someone who knows someone who knows someone who . . .', 'an influential acquaintance in the right place'. *Se faire pistonner* is everyone's cherished hope (*v.* also RELATIONS).

placé. The word which should come to mind when you need to express 'in a position' (to do, know, help, or whatever). *Il est mieux placé que moi pour vous renseigner.* 'He's in a better position than I am to inform you.' *Demandez-le-lui, il est bien placé pour le savoir.* 'Ask him; he should know.'

plaque minéralogique (f). 'The license' or 'number plate' of a car. The last two digits tell you which *département* the car comes from: 75 for Paris (la Seine), 33 for Bordeaux (la Gironde), and so on.

plein. *En plein* is a good way to translate 'in the midst of'—*en plein travail* ('absorbed in work', 'in the midst of working'), *en pleine croissance* ('in the midst of growth'), *en plein dedans* (*J'ai voulu éviter cette flaque d'eau mais je suis tombé en plein dedans*—'I wanted to avoid that puddle but I fell smack into it'). This is not, however, 100 per cent reliable: *en plein air* is not 'in mid-air', but 'in the open (air)'; 'in mid-air' would be *dans l'air*.

You know that *il a la bouche pleine de chocolat* means 'his mouth is full of chocolate', and that *plein* here has to be feminine, since it modifies *la bouche*. But you can turn the expression around: *il a du chocolat* (or *de la glace*) *plein la bouche*, in which case *plein* is an adverb, and invariable, no matter what precedes or follows, as in . . . *plein les poches*.

plomb (m). 'An electric fuse'; but *quand le plomb a sauté*, 'when the fuse has blown', you do not call *le plombier*! He's 'the plumber'; and it's *l'électricien* you want.

pochette (f). Not only 'a small pocket', but also a couple of the articles which you can slip into a pocket: a man's breast-pocket handkerchief, and a book of matches. Also 'the card-board sleeve' of a gramophone record. 'The paper jacket' of a hardcover book is *une jaquette*.

poêle (f. and m.). One of those hermaphrodite words, like *mode*, *vase*, *voile*, which change meanings along with their gender. *La poêle* is 'the frying pan', whereas *le poêle* is 'the heating apparatus': *un poêle à charbon, à gaz, à mazout*. Watch out for *poil* (m)—(*v.* CHEVEUX)—which, although pronounced similarly, has nothing to do with either *poêle*.

poinçonneur (m). Or, as is more often the case, *poinçonneuse* (f): the person who punches a hole in your Métro ticket.

point (m). *Etre sur le point de* is the first expression to be committed to memory: 'to be just about to'. *Il était sur le point de sortir quand nous sommes arrivés.* 'He was just going out when we arrived.'

Next, 'to point at someone' is not *'pointer'* but *montrer quelqu'un* (*du bout*) *du doigt, l'indiquer du doigt*. And if you want to say to someone 'you've got a point there!' you'd best say *il y a du vrai dans ce que vous dites!* Conversely, 'I don't see the point (of what you're saying)' is *Je ne vois pas où vous voulez en venir*.

Se pointer is, colloquially, 'to show up'. *Normalement il arrive avec un retard monstre, mais ce matin il s'est pointé à l'heure.* 'Usually he comes in awfully late, but this morning he showed up on time.'

Faire le point, like *récapituler*, is an expression to which the moderator of a discussion may have recourse: *faisons le point*, 'let's sum up'.

Au point où nous en sommes (*où il en est* etc.), *autant* . . . is a good way of rendering 'since we've gone this far, we might just as well . . .' *Mettre quelque chose au point* is 'to perfect something *or* see to the details of it'.

poisson rouge (m). 'Goldfish'!

ponctuation (f). You are certainly beyond the *dictée* stage by now, but one can never be too sure of one's punctuation.

> *Une virgule*, 'comma'.
> *Un point virgule*, 'semicolon'.
> *Un point*, 'period', 'full stop'. (*Un point, c'est tout*, said in a tone of firm finality, means 'period, that's all', 'that's my last word'.)
> *Deux points*, 'colon'.
> *Point à la ligne*, 'end of the preceding sentence and start a new paragraph' (*un paragraphe*).
> *Un point d'interrogation*, 'question mark'.
> *Un point d'exclamation*, 'exclamation mark'.
> *Une apostrophe*, 'apostrophe'.
> *Un tiret*, 'dash'.
> *Un trait d'union*, 'hyphen'.
> *Entre crochets*, 'in brackets'.
> *Entre parenthèses*, 'in parentheses', or 'parenthetically'.
> *Ouvrir* (*fermer*) *une parenthèse*, 'beginning (end) of parenthesis'.
> *Trois points de suspension*, 'ellipsis', as . . .
> *Entre guillemets*, 'in quotes *or* quotation marks'. *Ouvrir* (*fermer*) *les guillemets*, 'beginning (end) of quote'. You will have noticed already that in French, quotation marks are used less than in English and in a different way. A person's words are introduced by a dash and not by quotes at all, except in the case of consecutive paragraphs of the same person's speech. For instance: 'I will go,' he said, 'tomorrow.' —*J'irai, dit-il, demain.*

pont (m). 'A long holiday weekend'; i.e. one which bridges the holiday itself, *le jour férié*, and the nearest weekend. *Faire le pont*, when Christmas or some other holiday is on a Thursday, is to have the Friday off as well, making it a four-day weekend.

porte-. Like *coupe-* (q.v.), this can prefix almost anything that in English is likely to be followed by '-holder', '-rack', or '-case', and many other items as well: *un porte-clés, un porte-cigarettes, un porte-tasses . . . Un porte-manteau* is no stranger to you, but in French it means 'a clothes rack'; the sort of valise called 'portmanteau' in English is simply *une valise*. *Un portefeuille* is not so much 'a portfolio' (which is *un porte-documents*) as 'a wallet (US: 'billfold')', while *un porte-monnaie* is 'a change purse', in which you may sometimes carry bank notes too. *Un porte-parole*, literally 'a word-carrier', is 'a spokesman'. On the same principle, you build words such as *un presse-papiers*, 'a paperweight'; and *des serre-livres*, 'book ends.'

portion (f). 'A helping' or 'serving' of food (*v.* SERVIR).

pose (f). The installation of something you've bought, such as carpeting or wallpaper. When you go to buy it, you'll find two prices: *au rouleau* (or *au mètre*), and *avec la pose*. Furniture stores and decorators will often advertise *livraison et pose à domicile*, 'delivery to and installation in your home'.

Posé, when said of a person or of a person's voice, means 'calm', 'poised', 'under control'.

The verb *poser* ought to be paired off in your mind with *demander*, since 'to ask (for) something' is *demander quelque chose*, while 'to ask a question' is *poser une question*.

pot (m). Included here to remind you of:

dîner à la fortune du pot, 'to take pot luck';

prendre un pot, 'to have a drink'; quite *familier*, but you must know it, as you're bound to meet with it at least once a day. *Passez à la maison prendre un pot*. 'Drop in and have a drink';

manque de pot! 'Tough luck!' 'Too bad!' A good deal more casual than *dommage!*;

pot-de-vin (m), 'a bribe'.

Notice that *un pot* is not only 'a pot' but 'a jar' as well—*un pot de confiture, de yaourt*(or *yogourt*), *de moutarde*, and so forth; it may also be called *un verre*. *Pot perdu* marked on the bottom of the jar means that you pay no deposit on it (*v.* CONSIGNE). 'Kitchen pots and pans' are called *casseroles* (f).

pourboire (m). 'A tip' *pour boire*, 'to buy a drink', the silver with which you cross someone's palm in gratitude for services rendered or in anticipation of services requested. An inescapable angle of daily life in France as virtually anywhere else. The *chauffeur du taxi* will tell you the fare without adding the tip to it himself, which leaves it up to you to figure out 10% or 15% and to hand it over. The rule of at least 10% and more often 15% generally holds good; certainly nothing less is acceptable. *L'ouvreuse* ('the usherette') at the cinema expects it; the boy who gets your car out of the garage expects it; *le coiffeur* expects at least that. A restaurant usually makes sure of it by adding it to the fixed price of the menu: *service compris*. If you don't see this marked on the menu and you're not sure from the looks of the bill whether it's been done, it is legitimate to ask *le garçon* or *la caissière*: *Est-ce que le service est compris?* Restaurants may have another guarantee in this field: you pay for *le couvert*—the fork, knife and spoon, and the plate you eat from—a nominal sum, usually the first item on the menu and on the bill.[1] Often, in a little restaurant, if there are any *serviettes* ('napkins') at all, they come in two price groups: *cellulose* ('paper'), which is less, and *toile* or *tissu*, which is more of a luxury.

---

[1] *En principe*, a government decree early in 1966 abolished this practice.

Your *concierge* expects it, under the name of *étrennes* (q.v.) at New Year's time, and you'd best count at least 10F per person in your family. Your *facteur* ('postman') collects it at the same time of year by coming around to sell you a wall calendar, which you buy for, let us say, 3 or 5 francs.

poursuivre, se. Literally, 'to follow *or* to chase oneself'; so—'to go on', 'to continue' or 'to be continued'. *Les négociations se poursuivront la semaine prochaine.* 'The talks will be continued next week.'

poussière (f). 'Dust', of course; 'to dust', *épousseter.* 'The dustbin' or 'garbage pail' is *la boîte à ordures*, or *la poubelle*; and 'the garbage man' is *l'éboueur.*

Avoir une poussière dans l'œil, 'to have grit in the eye'.

Poussières, in the plural, is used when telling time or counting money to express informally 'and the odd bit', 'a couple of minutes past', or whatever the case may be. *Il doit être deux heures et des poussières. Il ne me reste plus que treize francs et des poussières.*

presbyte. Nothing to do with 'presbytery', which is *le presbytère*, but with eyesight, since this is the word for 'farsighted'; the condition is *la presbytie.* The opposite, 'nearsightedness', is *la myopie*, and the adjective is *myope.*

You have to be careful with the word 'eyesight' itself, which in English is also called 'vision'; you have to say *la vue*, as *la vision* is not generally used for the physical capacity (*v.* VUE).

présenter. The verb you want for 'to introduce'. *Monsieur le Préfet, permettez-moi de vous présenter Mme Unetelle. Faire les présentations* is 'to do the introductions', 'do the honors'. *Introduire quelqu'un*, however, is 'to show someone in' (to a room, *dans la salle*), while *introduire quelque chose* is 'to insert something': *introduisez une pièce de vingt centimes dans la fente*, 'insert a twenty-centime piece into the slot'. *Présenter* is followed by *à* (*j'ai présenté ma mère à la sienne*, 'I introduced my mother to his'), and *introduire* by *dans.*

prévention (f). May be a *Faux Ami* to you, as it means 'prejudice', like *préjugé* (m) and *parti pris* (m). *Il a une prévention contre les rousses.* 'He's got a prejudice against redheads.' *La prévention routière* does, however, mean 'road safety'.

'Prevention' may be translated by *empêchement* (m), but this is often got around by *le fait d'empêcher*, *d'éviter*, or some such *formule.*

primordial. As in English, it means 'prime', 'primary', 'fundamental', but is used a good deal more often: *la chose primordiale*, or *c'est d'une importance primordiale.*

prise (f). The fact of taking, as in *une prise de contact* (*Nos conversations n'ont encore donné aucun résultat mais elles ont au moins servi de prise de contact.* 'Our talks have not yielded any result but at least they have allowed us to meet.'); *une prise de* *position*, 'a statement of opinion', the fact of taking a stand; and *la prise de conscience des grands problèmes de notre temps*, 'awareness of (awakening to) the great problems of our era'.

Une prise is also an 'electric plug' (*v.* BRANCHER).

prochain. It is well to bear in mind that this means not only 'next' as in a succession of things (*la prochaine fois*, 'next time'), but also 'immediately forthcoming' or 'imminent'. So, *Jean m'a fait part de son prochain mariage* does not necessarily mean that Jean has already been married and is about to re-marry, but merely that he is about to be married soon. Cinemas will advertise: *prochainement*—'coming soon'.

If you need to express 'next' *or* 'then' when telling a story, you need *ensuite* or *puis*: 'next, he knocked at the house next door', *ensuite il frappa à la maison d'à côté*. 'The lady next door' is simply *la voisine*, or *la dame qui habite à côté*. And when you are standing in line or sitting in the doctor's waiting room, the next person's turn will be announced by *au suivant* or *la personne suivante!*, since *le prochain*, as a noun, is 'one's neighbor' in the Biblical sense. *Il faut aimer son prochain*. 'Love your neighbor.' But you're quite safe in using the adjective *prochain* for the 'next' time, the 'next' train, the 'next' meeting, and so on.

produire, se. A verb which is not likely to occur to you at first when you want to express 'to happen' or 'occur' or 'take place'; and yet it is used as often as *se passer*. *Qu'est-ce qui s'est produit* (or *s'est passé*)? 'What happened?' *Je venais juste de rentrer quand il s'est produit une violente explosion*. 'I had just come home when a violent explosion occurred.'

Like *se manifester*, *se produire* can also mean 'to appear', 'to show up' and 'to make a stage appearance'.

professeur (m). Not only 'the university professor' but also 'the secondary-school master *or* teacher', as distinct from *l'instituteur* (*-trice*) or *le maître* (*-esse*), 'the elementary-school teacher'.

This seems to be as good a place as any to look at some of the terms which loom largest in the pupil's or the student's vocabulary without getting into their slang, which is infinite and changing.

admissible, être: 'to have passed a written exam' in a university successfully; this gives you the right—and the obligation—'to attempt the oral', *se présenter à l'oral*. *Un bi-admissible* is the candidate for the *Agrégation* (the ultimate in university *concours*) who has been lucky enough to pass the written exam twice, in two different years, but has not yet *réussi l'oral*. *Bi-admissible* is considered quite a worthy title in itself.

baccalauréat (m), abbreviated *bac* or *bachot*. The examination which signifies completion of secondary studies and allows a pupil to become a university student;

bizuther: 'to haze' a new student in one of the *grandes écoles*; these schools are on the level of the *facultés*, or beyond, but entrance is determined by a *concours*;

chahuter: 'to be rowdy in class', 'to heckle *or* create a disturbance';

collège (m): you may be misled by the British or American use of the term 'college'. In France this is 'a private secondary school', as distinct from the State *lycée* (m);

coller: 'to fail a student in his exam'; *être collé*, 'to fail';

composition (f): a 'term exam' in secondary school;

concours (m): 'competitive exam';

consigne or *colle* (f): 'punishment'; especially, being kept in on Thursday or Saturday;

faculté (f) or *fac*: 'college' of a university. *Faculté des Lettres et Sciences Humaines*, *Faculté de Médecine*, *Faculté de Droit*;

matière (f): 'subject of study', as '*philo*,' '*les maths*', etc.;

mention (f): 'special praise on an exam', 'honors', ranging from *Assez Bien* to *Bien* to *Très Bien*;

merde à la puissance 13!: distinctly a student way of saying 'good luck!';

moyenne (f): a passing grade or mark, *10 sur 20* or *20 sur 40*, since *examens* and *dissertations* are marked on the basis of 20, not of 100 or of A, B etc. A grade of 20 is unheard of; 18 places a student in an awesomely rarefied atmosphere; 15 is very respectable indeed;

polycopié (m): a mimeographed copy of a university professor's lectures;

promotion (f): the year of one's graduating class in a *faculté* or, especially, in a *grande école*;

reçu, être: 'to pass one's examination';

thème (m): 'translation from one's own language into a foreign one';

version (f): 'translation from the foreign tongue into one's own'.

propre (m). *C'est du propre!* corresponds to 'what a dirty trick!' Said with a certain indignant vehemence, it means the opposite of what it would seem to, since the adjective *propre* itself means 'clean', 'right', 'decent', 'fitting'. One washing-machine company made a neat play on words by claiming that its machine was *le propre du propre*, the very nature of cleanliness.

Propre can also mean, of course, 'own'; and you can remember this together with *le propriétaire*, 'owner', and *la propriété*, 'property'. ('To own', however, is *posséder*.) *Chacun croit que ses propres enfants sont des merveilles*. 'Everyone thinks his own children are wonderful.' Beware of mixing up *la propriété*, 'property' and *la propreté*, 'cleanliness'. The English word, 'propriety', is best translated by *les convenances* or *la bienséance*.

province (f). Anything outside Paris. This would seem simple
enough; but in order to understand the first thing about
France, from housing to traffic to culture, you must remember
to what extent France is still centered on Paris and realize
the indifference that some Parisians can put into the terms
province, *provincial*, *provincialisme* (m). (There is, however,
a healthful tendency towards *décentralisation* in all fields.)
Cette fille ne connaît rien en dehors de sa petite province—she's
a real rustic. *Débarquer de la province*, 'to come up from the
provinces', 'to leave the farm'. *Monter à Paris* is the aim of
many a career, whose consummation is the appointment to a
post in Paris. *Provincial*, adjective and noun, is not to be confused with *la Provence* and the adjective, *provençal*.

Q

quart (m). The fourth part of anything: *un quart de vin*, 'one fourth
of a litre of wine' (just over half a pint); *un quart de Reblochon*,
'a quarter of a round Reblochon cheese'; 'a quarter of an
hour'. *Il est dix heures un quart*, 'it's 10.15'.
 A mechanism—a car, for instance—*qui marche au quart de
tour* is one which works admirably well.

quartier (m). 'Neighborhood' or 'area' of a city. *Le quartier
estudiantin*, 'the student quarter'. Also, 'a section' of an
orange!

quasiment. 'Nearly', 'just about'; can be used as excessively and
as loosely as 'practically' is by some people in English: *il était
quasiment mort*, *c'était quasiment impossible*, and the like.

que. A few special uses of *que* which your grammar book may not
stress: Exclamatory: 'how many!' 'how much!' 'how long!'
'how!' *Que de choses ravissantes dans cette boutique!* 'What a lot
of lovely things in this shop!'
 Optative—requiring a subjunctive: *Qu'elle m'obéisse cette
fois ou je la renvoie!* 'She shall obey me this time or I shall
dismiss her!'
 'If only', 'what a pity' etc., as in these words attributed, in a
Figaro Littéraire of early March 1965 to Lord Attlee speaking of Churchill: *Que n'a-t-il pu vivre cent ans!* 'If only he
could have lived to be a hundred!'

quelconque. A very common way of expressing 'so-so', 'barely
tolerable'. *Normalement elle se montre excellente cuisinière,
mais ce soir, la soupe était quelconque.* 'Usually she's a splendid
cook, but the soup tonight was only so-so.'

quelque chose (m). The gender is worth noticing. 'A thing' is feminine, *une chose*; yet 'something' is masculine, *un quelque chose. Il a un petit quelque chose qui ne me plaît point.* 'There's something about him I don't care for at all.'

quelque part. 'Somewhere'. *Aller quelque part* is a common euphemism for 'going to the lavatory', which may also be called *au petit coin, aux toilettes, aux lavabos* (*v.* also CABINET, LAVABO).

The best way to ask in a café or restaurant is *où sont les toilettes?* In a private home, you may think you're being ultra-euphemistic by asking *où est la salle de bains?*, but be forewarned: especially in a pre-World War II house, the toilet is virtually never to be found in the bathroom but always apart.

Qui Vous Savez. Or *Qui Nous Savons.* 'You Know Who'; specifically, in the context of political cartoons since 13 May, 1958, General de Gaulle.

quoi. Apart from the obvious uses of *quoi*—'which', 'what'— you'll hear it used at the end of a sentence, for emphasis, as 'what' or 'wot' used to be in English. This sort of turn of phrase is definitely casual, all right when used by students among students, but it's very easy to overdo it and so to become, perhaps unintentionally, ripe for parody. Think of the fad, just a few years ago, for sticking 'like' on to the end of almost every other sentence. *On est sorti hier, comme ça, quoi, histoire de s'amuser un peu, quoi, on voulait voir un film, un truc drôle, quoi* . . . You see?

Il n'y a pas de quoi is quite polite, however, and like *de rien* and *je vous en prie*, means 'it's nothing', 'you're welcome', 'don't mention it.'

Il y a de quoi is rather like *et pour cause: il s'est mis en colère, il y a de quoi!* 'He got angry, who wouldn't? *or*, for good reason!'

R

radin. 'Miserly' or 'stingy'. Like *près de ses sous*, this adjective is more colloquial than is *avare*. You might expect, by analogy with *malin—maligne*, that the feminine form of *radin* would be '*radigne*', but no, *radine. Le radinisme* is the noun.

radio (f). 'An X-ray.' Or 'the wireless' (US: 'radio'). But 'a wireless set' is *un poste de radio*. So you should say *Je viens d'acheter un poste de radio*, and definitely not '. . . *une radio*'. The same thing is valid for television: *la télévision* is the system, and *le poste de télévision*, the receiving set. *La télé* is the abbreviation which corresponds to 'TV' or 'telly' in English. 'To hear something on the wireless *or* the radio' is

entendre quelque chose à la radio. 'To see something on television', *voir quelque chose à la télévision.*

raffoler. 'To love' or 'adore' something. *Les haricots verts? J'en
raffole!* 'French beans? I love them!' Intransitive, as you can
see: *raffoler de quelque chose.*

   (*S'*)*affoler* is 'to become excited' in a more violent way, 'to
panic', 'lose one's wits'. *Calmez-vous, il n'y a pas de quoi
s'affoler.* 'Calm down, there's no need to get all excited.'

rafistoler. 'To mend', 'patch', 'fix up any old way'; more colloquial than *raccommoder, arranger,* or *réparer,* and the sort of
work involved is usually more sketchy. *Le rafistolage* is the
noun.

rapporter. You're likely to hear this used most often as meaning
'to yield', 'to be lucrative *or* profitable', *être intéressant (v.*
INTÉRÊT). *Le rapport* can be 'profit'; or 'a report'—although
'a news reporter' is *un reporter* or *un journaliste,* and 'his
coverage' is *son reportage*—or the connection or relationship
between any two or more things or persons. *Je ne vois pas le
rapport,* 'I don't get the connection'. *Cela n'a aucun rapport.*
'That has nothing to do with it ' (*v.* also VOIR).

rapprocher. Not to be confused with *reprocher. Rapprocher* is 'to
draw near to' (*de*), 'reconcile', 'bring together': *un rapproche-
ment Est-Ouest est à souhaiter.* 'A reconciliation of East and
West would be desirable.' *Se rapprocher de son but,* 'to
approach one's goal'.

   On the other hand *reprocher* (*à*) is 'to reproach'; and the
noun, *reproche,* is masculine. *Elle n'arrête pas de faire des
reproches à son mari.* 'She is everlastingly blaming her husband
for something.'

ras du cou. 'Crew-necked', or 'round-necked', for a pullover;
in contrast with *à col roulé,* 'turtle-necked'.

recharge (f). 'A refill' of a ball-point pen, a cigarette lighter, and
so forth. *Charger* is 'to load' (as *un fusil*) or 'fill'; *recharger,*
'to re-load' or 'refill'.

recommander. 'To recommend.' Note the difference in spelling:
the *e* at the end in English becomes *a,* just as in *correspondance*
(f), *indépendance* (f).

   And in post-office terms, 'to register': *une lettre recom-
mandée,* 'a registered letter'.

récurer. 'To scour', as in *une poudre qui récure, nettoie, fait briller*
—'a powder that scours, cleans, polishes'.

   But 'to scour', as a figure of speech—'I scoured the town
for a present for him'—cannot be translated by *récurer,* as we
once heard it attempted! *Faire toutes les boutiques, faire toute
la ville, chercher partout* would be more suitable, or *fouiller
(fureter par) toute la ville.*

réfléchir. 'To reflect', that is, 'to stop and think'. *Réflexion faite*, 'on second thoughts'. *Refléter* is 'to reflect' as in a mirror, and the noun is *un reflet*.

règlement (m). 'The rule', or 'the regulation'. *Il faut agir selon les règlements*. 'You must act according to the rules.'

Il n'a pas voulu porter l'uniforme réglementaire. 'He refused to wear the regulation uniform.'

Règlement can also be 'a payment', or 'squaring of an account'. The carpenter who has come to work for you will mark on the bottom of his bill, after the sum due, *en votre aimable règlement*—'which you will kindly pay!' *Un règlement de comptes* in the underworld means 'a session of getting even or wiping out a grudge'. *Régler sa note d'hôtel* is 'to pay one's hotel bill'.

Le règlement is not to be confused with *le réglage*, which is 'the regulating' or 'adjusting' of a mechanical apparatus.

When a decision is to be made and an external factor suddenly intervenes, obviating the need to decide, you say *Comme cela, la question est réglée!* 'That's done it!' 'That settles it!'

Avoir (mettre) ses papiers en règle, 'to have (put) one's papers in order'.

rejeton (m). This may look like a strange term for 'child' or 'offspring', but there it is. One young woman, hearing the word for the first time and applied, by a friend at that, to her own child, was incensed, feeling that there was something pejorative about it. *Rejeton* is simply a good deal more *familier* than *enfant*.

relations (f. pl.). 'Valuable connections', people in a position to wangle things for you. *On a beau avoir beaucoup de diplômes, si on n'a pas aussi beaucoup de relations.* 'Having a lot of degrees isn't enough, you've got to know people as well' (*v.* also PISTON).

Once again, *relations* does not mean 'relatives' (*v.* PARENT).

religieuse (f). 'A nun', formerly called *une nonne*, now more commonly *une (bonne) sœur* as well.

Also a certain type of pastry.

remise (f). 'A discount' on the price of an article: *une forte remise*, 'a big discount'. *Un rabais* is also 'a reduction', but a *rabais* is not *fort*, it is *gros*.

Also 'a shed' or 'a shack' behind the main house, as 'a tool shed'.

La remise is also 'the postponement' of something, since one of the many meanings of *remettre* is 'to postpone'. *Ne remettez jamais au lendemain ce que vous pouvez faire faire aujourd'hui par un autre.* 'Never put off until tomorrow what you can get someone else to do for you today.'

Remettre quelque chose en question is 'to bring something up all over again', 'lay it open for discussion again'.

rendre. You are familiar with *se rendre compte*, 'to realize'. *Je me suis rendu compte plus tard que j'aurais pu l'offenser*. 'Afterwards I realized that I might have offended him.'

Se rendre is 'to surrender'; the noun is *la reddition* or, more frequently, *la capitulation*.

But *se rendre* is also used, and quite often, where English uses simply 'to go'. *La Reine s'est rendue sur les lieux de la catastrophe*. 'The Queen visited the scene of the disaster.'

Rendre is used more readily for 'to translate' than is 'render' in English.

And since the basic meaning of *rendre* is 'to give back', *rendre* also colloquially renders the English 'to vomit'.

rente (f). Not usually the word for 'rent,' which is *le loyer*; 'to rent' or 'let' is *louer*. *Les rentes* are one's '(unearned) income', from stocks, annuities, and the like; *vivre de ses rentes*, 'to live on one's income'. *Mais c'est une rente!* 'But that's terribly dear (expensive)!'

reprendre. 'To pick up (the thread of something) again'; a useful substitute for *recommencer*. *Reprenons notre discussion*. 'Let's resume our discussion'. *Reprenons à la ligne cinq, voulez-vous bien?* 'Let's go back to line five, shall we?' Or, 'to point out mistakes'. *Il la reprend à chaque fois qu'elle fait une faute de grammaire*. 'He corrects her each time she makes a grammatical error.'

Also 'to take in'—a pair of trousers, a dress—as opposed to *donner*, 'to let out'.

retouche (f). 'An alteration' made in an article of clothing. Shops will often put up a sign to reassure you. *La maison se charge des retouches*. 'We take care of alterations.'

retourner. 'To upset someone emotionally', among other more obvious meanings. *La nouvelle de son départ m'a réellement retourné*. 'I was really upset on hearing that he'd gone away.' *Faire quelque chose (à quelqu'un)* is another away of saying the same thing: *ça m'a fait quelque chose*, 'it did something to me'.

retraite (f). 'A military *or* a religious retreat'; and also 'retirement'. *Prendre sa retraite* is 'to retire'; and the person who does so is *un(e) retraité(e)*. *Toucher sa retraite* is 'to receive one's pension'. 'To retire' or 'withdraw' from the room, however, or from the world, is *se retirer (de)*.

réveillon (m). A very essential word in the last week of December: the Christmas Eve celebration and again, the New Year's Eve (*la Saint Sylvestre*) party. In either case, wining, dining, dancing, and noise-making. The 'done' thing is either to go to *un réveillon* at some friends' or to go out to a restaurant or two. It is wise to book ahead. Some days beforehand, cafés and restaurants will chalk up *Réveillon* on their windows and announce their featured attractions if there is to be a show. The verb is *réveillonner*.

rêveur (m). Included here for the sake of *cela laisse rêveur*: 'it makes you stop and think', or 'it gives you something to think about'. Said of any sort of impressive situation, enviable or chilling. *Au début il était simple employé; à présent c'est le grand patron. Cela laisse rêveur.* 'In the beginning he was a mere employee; now he's the big boss. Food for thought there.'

rideau (m). 'A curtain', theatrical or otherwise; *le Rideau de Fer*, 'the Iron Curtain'.

   Also, the veritable 'iron curtain' incorporated into all self-respecting old fireplaces and lowered like a portcullis to hide the blackened hearth or to make the chimney draw better when a fire is going.

risquer. It may take you a while to get used to the idea that this verb does not necessarily imply danger, as it does in English. *S'il continue sur sa lancée, il risque fort de réussir.* 'If he goes on at that rate, he's got a good chance of making good'' *Nous risquons gros*, 'we're taking a big risk', 'a lot is at stake'. 'A risk' is *un risque*.

rondelet(te). The equivalent of 'well padded', or 'chubby,' when speaking of a person. Less diplomatic than *(être) bien en chair*. *Boulot(te)* is a less polite word — 'short and fat'. *Une somme rondelette* is a tidy little sum.

ronéotyper. A process for reproducing typed pages; corresponds in appearance to mimeographing.

rouspéter. A much-used verb in this land of *l'individu*, as it means 'to protest', 'to complain'. *Un rouspéteur* is the person who does so.

roux (rousse). 'Red- *or* auburn-haired'. You never say that someone has *'les cheveux rouges'*!—he has *les cheveux roux. Une rousse* is 'an auburn-haired woman'. *Une tache de rousseur*, 'a freckle'.

S

S.A. *Société Anonyme*; corresponds to 'Company, Ltd.', or 'Company, Inc.'. *S.A.R.L.*, *Société Anomyme à Responsabilité Limitée.*

sage. One of the classic sources of confusion, as it can mean either 'good' (well-behaved) or 'wise'. Obviously when you say to a child *sois sage*, you're not saying, 'be wise', but 'be good', 'behave yourself'. Applied to grown-ups, *sage* and *la sagesse* generally have to do with wisdom—or with prudence, which of course is not too far removed from good behavior. *Autrefois il buvait énormément, à présent il a décidé d'être sage.* 'He used to drink an awful lot; now he's turned over a new leaf.' *S'assagir* is 'to become good', 'behave better'.

Une sage-femme, to be encountered a good deal more often in France than in the US or England, is 'a midwife'.

saisir. 'To seize' or 'grip' physically, like *attraper*; or mentally, like *comprendre* or sometimes, *suivre* (q.v.). *Qu'a-t-il dit? Je n'ai pas saisi.* 'What did he say? I didn't get (catch) it.'

The present participle, *saisissant,* is often used where it would never occur to an English-speaker to use 'seizing'. 'Striking', 'stunning', 'thrilling' is more like it.

saison, la belle. 'Summer'; the fine weather which is supposed to correspond to *les grandes vacances (scolaires),* from late June to late September. For all practical purposes, the month that really matters is August (*v.* FERMETURE ANNUELLE).

'To season food' is *assaisonner;* the noun is *un assaisonnement.*

salade (f). 'A salad'; also 'a lettuce', otherwise called *une laitue.* 'The salad bowl' is *le saladier.*

Also, colloquially, a rather dubious term, meaning 'a mess', 'a bad business' (*v.* also HISTOIRE). And *le panier à salade* is not only 'the salad shaker' but also 'the Black Maria'.

sandwich (m). Pronounced 'sandweech', even in the plural, which is written *sandwichs.*

sans façon. The nearest thing you'll find to 'informal', along with *simple, en toute simplicité,* and *sans cérémonie. Il est sans façon (sans cérémonie).* 'He's very informal'. *Elle nous a reçu en toute simplicité.* 'She welcomed us informally'.

Or *sans façon* can mean 'sincerely', 'really'. *Non merci, sans façon.* 'No thank you, really.'

saucisse (f). A sausage that needs cooking before it is eaten— *saucisse de Francfort, de Strasbourg* etc., as distinct from *saucisson* (m), already cooked and ready to be eaten cold— *saucisson d'Arles* etc. Also, a bread shaped like a *saucisson.*

Saucissonner is a disdainful term for the straightforward way in which many a French family will eat in the *compartiment* of a train or on a Sunday outing: a long loaf, a long sausage, a ripe Camembert, and a knife to cut it all up with.

sauter. 'To jump', 'leap', 'skip' and so forth. Also 'to explode' or 'go off'. *Faire sauter* is loosely used to mean not only 'to set off', but also 'to get rid of', *supprimer, faire disparaître. Faire sauter la cloison entre deux pièces,* 'to get rid of the partition between two rooms'.

Ça saute aux yeux (or, less properly, *ça crève les yeux*) is literally 'it's staring you in the face'; in other words, 'it's obvious'.

sauver, se. A dramatic-looking verb but one which can be—and often is—used for something as everyday as 'I must be going': *je dois me sauver. Il s'est sauvé avant la fin du concert.* 'He slipped out before the end of the concert.'

savant (m). As a noun, 'scholar' and almost exclusively, 'scientist' —who, by the way, is never a *'scientiste'* but *un homme de science*. And as an adjective, not only 'scholarly' but 'knowing', 'clever', 'expert'. *Avec des gestes savants, elle se coiffa,* 'deftly, she combed her hair'.

savoir. One *formule* with which you absolutely must be familiar is *je ne veux pas le savoir,* a nearly-universal way of putting an end to an argument or to opposition from someone. You might translate 'that's no concern of mine', 'that's your problem', 'that's your tough luck', or something along those lines. —*Il est impossible de terminer ce rapport pour vendredi.* —*Je ne veux pas le savoir, il me le faut!* 'It's impossible to finish this report by Friday.' 'That's not my problem, I've got to have it.'

Another is *être payé pour savoir quelque chose,* 'to know something all too well'. *Attention, c'est un escroc, je suis payé pour le savoir.* 'Watch out, he's a crook, as I learned to my sorrow.' Similar to *faire les frais de quelque chose, faire l'expérience de quelque chose.*

séduire. Can be less limited and dramatic than 'seduce' in English; and the same holds true, of course, for *séduisant, séduction, séducteur (-trice).* The idea is that of general attraction or temptation. An airline company advertised its *formule séduisante* for round-the-world trips, meaning its attractive price scales.

sélectionner. 'To choose' or 'select'; *fruits sélectionnés,* for instance, are 'choice *or* select fruit'. The idea is that the choice aims at quality. Merely 'to sort', as such, is *trier, faire un tri.*

semblant. Included here to warn you off *prétendre,* when you mean 'to pretend', 'to make believe'; *faire semblant* is needed in that case. *Prétendre* means 'to claim' or 'to have claims (upon something)', as 'a pretender to the throne'—*un prétendant*—should help you to remember.

sens (m). 'Sense', 'meaning', 'signification'. *Cette phrase n'a pas de sens (est un non-sens).* 'This sentence is meaningless.' *C'est insensé,* 'it's sheer madness'.

'Direction'. *Prenez dans ce sens-là, vous tomberez sur la Concorde.* 'Go in that direction, you'll land right in the Place de la Concorde.'

A perceptive faculty: *la vue, l'odorat, l'ouïe, le toucher, le goût*—'sight', 'smell', 'hearing', 'touch', 'taste'. *Avoir un sixième sens,* 'to have a sixth sense'.

sens dessus-dessous. 'Upside-down'; and *'dessous-dessus'* won't do, any more than 'downside-up' will in English! You might expect 'inside out' to work analogously, but no: *à l'envers* is the answer, *l'endroit* (m) being 'the "right" side', and *l'envers* (m) 'the "wrong" side'. *Mettre à l'endroit*, 'to turn right side out'—or 'right side up', since *à l'envers* also means 'upside-down'.

serpillière (f). 'A wet mop' for floors.

service (m). A few phrases to be noted with special care:

Service (non) compris, 'tip (not) included'; something you should watch for on the menu (*v.* POURBOIRE).

Rendre service (à quelqu'un), 'to do (someone) a favor'. Or, in place of *être utile*, 'to be useful'. *Cette table m'a bien rendu service.* 'I found that table very useful.' *Ça pourrait toujours rendre service.* 'It could always come in handy.'

Le service d'ordre, 'the police'.

Faire son service militaire, 'to do one's national (military) service'.

servir. 'To serve', 'to be useful'; 'to help someone (at table)'. *Servez-vous de petits pois.* 'Help yourself to peas.' *A quoi ça sert?* (or, more correctly, *à quoi cela sert-il?*). 'What's the good in (doing) that?' 'What's the use?' Or, in the case of an object, 'what's it for?', 'what's it supposed to be used for?' *Serviable*, 'cooperative', 'helpful' (*v.* ARRANGER).

si. The emphatic 'yes', as you know, particularly the 'yes' which contradicts a negative. *—Vous n'y pensez pas! —Mais si!* 'You're not seriously thinking of doing that!' 'Oh yes, I am!' It may be used for polite insistence: *—Je ne peux pas accepter ce prêt. —Mais si mais si, je vous en prie.* 'I can't accept this loan.' 'Nonsense, I insist.' And of course there's nothing at all surprising about *Si si si si si . . .* Where you stop is up to you.

Colloquially, you can make use of *si?* as a query, replacing *n'est-ce pas?*, with the aim of confirming a negative sentence. *Il ne vient pas, si?* 'He's not coming, or is he?'

Si also means 'if'. Used in a certain way it becomes a rhetorical or explanatory 'if' which approximates to 'because'. *Si je me permets de vous le signaler, c'est que . . .* 'I'm taking the liberty of pointing this out to you because . . .'

siège (m). 'The seat'—of a car or any other vehicle, of a person, or loosely, 'a chair'. *Prenez un siège.* 'Have a seat.' The exception is the seat you have at the theatre or at the cinema, which is *un fauteuil* or *une place*. 'To get a ticket', or 'book a seat', *louer une place*.

Le siège social of a political party, business firm, or other organization is its 'headquarters' or 'head office'; 'a military headquarters', however, is *le quartier général*. *Siéger*, 'to sit', 'be in session'. And *le Saint Siège* is 'the Holy See'.

signaler. Very often used with the idea of *faire remarquer*: 'to indicate', 'point out', or 'underline'. *Je tiens seulement à vous* *signaler que . . .* 'I simply want to point out to you that . . .' *Le signalement* of a person is the list of his distinguishing (physical) characteristics, especially of *un homme recherché par la police*, 'a wanted man'. *La signalisation* is 'the system of road signs'.

sinistre (m). A term which may catch you off balance, since it does not mean 'a sinister person', but 'a grave accident' or 'natural catastrophe'—earthquake, fire, and so forth, and *les sinistrés* are 'the victims' of the catastrophe.

As an adjective, *sinistre* is straightforward enough, meaning what 'sinister' does in English.

souffrant. Can be less painful than 'suffering', since it often means simply 'sick' or 'ill', and is considered more polite than the term *malade. J'espère que votre mère n'est plus souffrante.* 'I hope your mother is well now.' But *la souffrance* does mean 'suffering' or 'pain', and cannot express 'illness', for which you need *la maladie* or *l'affection* (*du foie*—of the liver etc.). 'A sick person' or 'a patient' is *un(e) malade*, and if you want to wish someone a quick recovery, you send *vos vœux de prompt rétablissement.*

sous. Generally 'under', 'below', 'sub-' (*un sous-marin*); but often needing a different translation in expressions where English uses 'within', 'in', 'at', 'before', and other prepositions. *Sous le règne de Louis XIV*, 'in the reign of Louis XIV'; *sous huitaine*, 'within the week'; *sous la main* 'before one's eyes' or 'ready at hand'.

stage (m). Not 'a theatrical stage', which is *la scène*, but 'a period of training *or* apprenticeship', with or without a course. A secretarial school student will *faire un stage comme dactylo chez un fabricant, un éditeur* etc.—work as a trainee typist for a manufacturer, a publisher, and so on. The trainee is *un(e) stagiaire.*

strapontin (m). 'Folding seat' in the aisle of a theatre or public vehicle.

suivre. 'To follow'; and especially, 'to understand'. *Excusez-moi, je ne vous suis pas.* 'I'm sorry, I don't follow you'.

'To take': *suivre un cours de géographie.* 'To take a geography course.' 'To take care of': *C'est le même médecin qui la suit depuis dix ans.* 'She's been going to the same doctor for ten years.'

Faire suivre son courrier, 'to have one's mail forwarded'. On the envelope you mark *Faire suivre (en cas de départ)*. 'Please forward if necessary.'

Lire la suite à la page 12, at the bottom of a newspaper article, tells you that it is 'continued on page 12'. Conceivably, you could ask to *écouter la suite de la suite No. 5*—'to listen to the rest of the fifth suite'.

Avoir de la suite dans les idées, 'to be consistent *or* logical'.

surenchérir. 'To raise the bid' at *une vente aux enchères*, 'an auction'; and by extension, 'to outbid someone' in conversation by over-emphasizing what has already been said, making redundant remarks.

système (m). 'System', of course; and also, more loosely, 'set-up', 'business', 'the works'. *Il a tenu absolument à me montrer son bureau—tapis, classeurs, tout le système.* 'He insisted on showing me his office—rug, filing cabinets, the works.'

Il me tape sur le système is quite a slangy way of saying 'I can't stand him'.

And of course you must not forget the justly famous *Système D* (*v.* DÉBROUILLER).

T

tabac (m). Either 'tobacco', or 'the tobacconist's'. If the latter, *un tabac* is generally *un café* at the same time, distinguishable from the *cafés* which are not *tabacs* by the traditional sign of the red carrot, since a roll of tobacco leaves used to be called *une carotte.* You can buy postage stamps as well in a tabac as *à la poste*; or *un billet* or *un dixième* (q.v.) *de la Loterie Nationale*, or *la vignette* (q.v.) for your car. Certain *tabacs* sell 'official *or* fiscal stamps': *des timbres fiscaux.*

tabatière (f). Called *un vasistas* as well, when it means the prop-up window in the severely gabled wall of many a sought-after *chambre de bonne.* In Paris, maid's rooms house fewer and fewer maids, and more and more students.

Une tabatière is also 'a snuffbox'; and *le tabac à priser*, 'snuff'.

table des matières (f). 'The table of contents' of a book. If you expect to find it at the beginning of the volume, you will look for it in vain, since it is generally placed at the end.

taille (f). Your 'height', your 'waist', and your 'size' in general. *Il est bien taillé.* 'He's well built.' *Il est de taille moyenne.* 'He's of average height.' *Il (elle) a la taille fine.* '(S)he is narrow-waisted.' *J'ignore son tour de taille.* 'I don't know his waist measurement.' In a shop: *quelle taille voulez-vous (prend-elle)?* 'What size are you looking for (does she wear)?' *Je voudrais la taille en dessus*: 'I'd like the next larger size'; *la taille en dessous*, 'the next smaller'. In the case of shoes, socks, stockings, and gloves, however, size is expressed not by *la taille* but by *la pointure*; and certain men's articles, pajamas and underclothes particularly, are measured by *patron*, 'medium'; *grand patron*, 'big'; and *demi-patron*, 'small' (*v.* PATRON).

Il n'est pas de taille à réussir cela. 'He's not up to (capable of) doing that successfully.'

tailleur (m). In spite of its gender, strictly 'a woman's suit', never a man's, which is *un costume*. *Une veste* is either a man's or a woman's 'jacket', and may be more *fantaisie*, 'non-classic'— in color, cut, and material—than *un veston*, which is always of cloth and always for men.

Needless to say, *un tailleur* is also the person responsible for the clothes: 'the tailor'.

tant. You might add to what your grammar book tells you about *tant*, these expressions: *Tant qu'à faire, autant . . .* 'While we're at (about) it, we might just as well . . . ' *Tant qu'à faire, autant tout faire refaire en même temps.* 'While we're at it, we might just as well have everything re-done at once.'

Tant et tant: 'such and such sum *or* amount'. *Mettons que je gagne tant et tant.* 'Supposing I earn such and such.'

And that curious expression (no use in trying to make sense of it word for word), *Vous m'en direz tant.* 'You've just said a mouthful', 'there's nothing left to add', might be adequate translations.

tapis (m). Generally speaking, this is 'a rug', Oriental or otherwise, as distinct from *un tapis cloué* or *une moquette*, which means '(wall-to-wall) carpeting'. *Une carpette*, contrary to what you might expect, is 'a small rug'; and so is *la descente de lit*, 'the small bedside rug'. *Un tapis de bain* is, none the less, 'a bathmat'.

La tapisserie is more likely nowadays to mean 'upholstery' than 'tapestry'; just as *un tapissier* is more likely to be 'an upholsterer'. And *tapisser les murs* is quite simply, 'to put on wallpaper', which is called *le papier peint*.

tel ou tel. 'Such and such a'. *Il nous racontait jusqu'aux moindres détails de son voyage, qu'il avait mangé dans tel ou tel restaurant, qu'il était descendu dans tel ou tel hôtel, et ainsi de suite.* 'He told us about his trip down to the smallest details, about eating in such and such a restaurant, staying at such and such an hotel, and so forth.'

tel quel. 'Just as it is' (they are, etc.). *Au lieu de ranger ses papiers, il les laisse toujours tels quels.* 'He just leaves his papers as they are, instead of putting them away.'

temple (m). '*A* Protestant church'—the building. *L'Eglise protestante* refers to '*the* Protestant Church', that is, the religion. 'A Jewish temple' is *une synagogue*.

tenir. Another of those multi-purpose verbs that often seem to go far afield from the basic meaning: 'to hold' or 'to keep'.

Il tient de son père. 'He's like his father.'

Je le tiens de lui. 'I have it (learnt it) from him'. 'He's the one who told me.'

Tenir en place, 'to stay still'. *A partir de 5h du soir, les élèves ne tiennent plus en place.* 'Past five in the evening, the pupils simply can't sit still.'

Tenir à quelque chose, 'to value something', 'care a great deal about it'. *Attention à ce vase, j'y tiens.* 'Be careful with that vase, it means a lot to me.'

S'en tenir à quelque chose, 'to put stock in something', 'to believe'. *Je ne sais plus à quoi m'en tenir.* 'I don't know what to believe any more.'

S'en tenir là, 'to be content with something', 'to refrain from going further'. *Tenez-vous-en là!* 'You'd better stop there!'

Tiens! or *Tenez!* 'Well' 'Hello!' 'Hey! What's this!' 'Just think!' etc.

Tenir debout, 'to ring true', 'to be plausible', said of a story. *Son histoire ne tient pas debout.* 'His version doesn't hold water, won't wash.'

terre-plein (m). In town, a paved square or the center strip of a boulevard or traffic circle; you may, sometimes, park your car on it.

tiquer. Among horses, to have a vicious habit of biting; and in human terms, by extension, 'to wince' or 'show one's reaction of annoyance'; and so, broadly, 'to be irked *or* displeased'. *Ce qui m'a toujours fait tiquer, c'est . . .* 'The thing that's always annoyed me is . . .'

tirer. Still another of those verbs that crop up everywhere:

S'en tirer, 'to manage' or 'muddle through'. *Il s'en tire à peu près.* 'He's just about getting along.' *Je ne m'en suis pas tiré si mal que ça.* 'I got out of it pretty well.'

Il n'y a rien à en tirer. 'It's (he's) a hopeless case; there's nothing to be done about it (him).'

Tirer quelque chose au clair, 'to bring something out into the open', 'to clarify something'.

Tirer les conclusions, 'to draw a conclusion'.

Tirer (toucher) à sa fin, 'to draw to a close'.

toc! A rather elastic little exclamation, expressing anything from 'knock knock!' on the door, to the recognition that a remark has struck home or the announcement of some event: 'there!' 'so there!' 'well said!' 'there it was!' or whatever the context calls for.

tomber. Gives rise to a number of expressions which, translated word for word, are quite comical:

Tomber à l'eau (said of a plan or idea), 'to fall through', 'not to work'. *Ses projets pour dimanche sont tombés à l'eau.* 'His plans for Sunday have fallen through.'

Tomber bien, 'to occur at the right moment'. *Tu tombes bien, nous nous mettons à table à l'instant.* 'You've come just at the right time; we were about to sit down to table.'

Tomber mal is, of course, just the opposite: 'to be inopportune'.

Tomber sur quelque chose, 'to find something directly', some-times with an element of surprise. *Je suis tombé sur sa maison du premier coup.* 'I found his house on the first try.'

Laisser tomber—anything, from a cup to an idea to a subject of conversation to a person—is 'to drop' or 'abandon'. (Although 'let's drop the subject' or 'let's change the subject' is *parlons d'autre chose*.)

Tomber (or *donner*) *dans le panneau* is a colloquial expression: 'to be taken in by something', 'to fall into a trap *or* for a trick'.

toqué. Said of an egg, or of a person, that is cracked. It is applied to the first more frequently in certain provinces than in Paris.

toujours. It is worth reminding yourself that *toujours* does not always means 'always', that is, 'forever and a day'. It can mean 'anyhow' or even 'just in case'. *Je ne crois pas que ça va marcher, mais essayez toujours.* 'I don't think it's going to work, but try anyhow (you can always try, there's no harm in trying).' Obviously not the same sort of *toujours* as in *vous êtes mon amour pour toujours*, or in *ils se connaissent depuis toujours*, 'they've known each other all their lives'.

tour, faire un. 'To go (come) out for a walk (*or* a ride)'. *Je vais juste faire un petit tour.* 'I'm just going out for a walk.' *Un tour en voiture*, 'a drive' or 'a ride'.

Not to be confused with *jouer un tour à quelqu'un*, 'to play a trick on someone'.

When *tour* changes gender, *une tour*, it means 'a tower'.

Toussaint (f). *La Toussaint* is 'All Saints' Day', 1 November; not a sad day in itself but immediately followed by *Le Jour des Morts* ('All Souls' Day'), 2 November—a day for placing wreaths on, and visiting, family graves.

tracasser, se. 'To worry' or 'fidget', like *s'en faire* or, in more formal terms, *s'inquiéter*. *Que de tracas!* 'Such a lot of problems!' *Ne vous tracassez pas!* 'Don't worry!'

Une tracasserie is less serious than *un tracas*.

traitement (m). 'Treatment', medical or otherwise; and also commonly used to mean 'salary'.

tranquille. What looks like a solely feminine form of the adjective is in fact the only one; and the *-ille* is pronounced like that in *ville*. *Etre tranquille* can mean not only 'to be quiet' but also 'to be alone', 'at ease', 'away from other people's noise or worries'. *Soyez tranquille, Monsieur, je m'en occupe.* 'You've nothing to worry about, sir, I'll take care of it.' *(Se) tran-quilliser* goes along with *(se) rassurer*. *Tranquillisez-vous*, 'calm down', 'rest assured'. *Un tranquillisant* is 'a tranquillizer'.

travailler. Chiefly 'to work', as you know. In a particular context, it can be used quite like *jouer*: 'to work', 'to warp'. And in another, colloquial one—*Qu'est-ce qui vous travaille?*—you have to translate by 'bother' or 'get': 'what's bothering you?'

(v. also TRACASSER, SE). But speaking of work, you must remember that *labourer* is definitely not a synonym for *travailler*, as *labourer* is 'to till the soil' or 'work the land'; and it follows that *un laboureur* is not any sort of worker in general but 'a tiller of the soil', 'farm laborer'. 'A worker' or 'laborer' is *un(e) ouvrier (ère)*, or sometimes *un travailleur*. Whereas *un travailliste* is a member of *le parti travailliste*, 'the Labor Party'.

traversin (m). The cylindrical pillow, or bolster, that goes across the width of the bed; very common in France, whether accompanied by the smaller square *oreiller* (m), 'pillow', or not.

tricolore (m). The French flag, *le drapeau tricolore*, whose colors are always listed in order, *bleu, blanc et rouge*, the opposite of the American and English 'red, white and blue'.

tromper. A notorious verb, as it means 'to be unfaithful in marriage': *tromper sa femme, tromper son mari*. Infidelity itself is *l'infidélité*.
  But you should not lose sight of the overall meaning, 'to deceive' or 'mislead'. *Se tromper*, logically enough, is 'to deceive oneself'; in other words, to be wrong or mistaken. And it follows that *trompeur* is the adjective you want for 'deceiving' or 'misleading', since *décevant*—from the verb, *décevoir*—is a *Faux Ami*, meaning 'disappointing'. Thus *quelle déception!* is 'what a disappointment!' while *quelle erreur!* means 'what a mistake!' 'how wrong he was!' etc.

trouvaille (f). 'A find', whether it be a 'buy', a lucky discovery, or a clever idea (v. also ASTUCE).

truc (m). A close cousin to *machin* (q.v.); but *truc* sometimes has the additional meaning of cleverness, 'a hint' or 'tip', *un machin astucieux. Elle m'a indiqué un truc pour réussir la mayonnaise.* 'She gave me a tip on making mayonnaise.' Definitely *familier*.
  Truquer is 'to fake', 'cheat', 'fraudulently alter'—*truquer une photo*.

tutoyer. To call someone '*tu*'. The big problem is when to do it and when not. The simplest answer is that you start out with *vous*, except with small children and domestic animals; then you wait to see how the situation and your personal taste evolve. Students, *entre eux*, use '*tu*' very readily. But in general the French, when conversing with or receiving a stranger, are far less casual and offhand than, for instance, Americans; so that to be called '*vous*', even after months or years of acquaintance, is not necessarily a sign of coldness. And you must remember that the plural of '*tu*' is '*vous*'; so, in case you think someone is being unnecessarily cold or standoffish in addressing you as '*vous*', stop first to think how many of you there are!

tuyau (m). A meaning which has become so widespread that it isn't even slang any more is that of 'a hint', 'a tip', 'a direct lead'—an extension of the basic meaning 'a pipe' or 'tube'. (*La tuyauterie de la salle de bains*, for instance, is the whole water pipe installation in the bathroom.) *Il cherche du travail et m'a demandé des tuyaux.* 'He's looking for work and asked me to give him some leads.'

U

une (f). The front page of a newspaper. *Cela mérite un gros titre à la une.* 'That's worth a big headline on page one.' A news program currently on French television is called *Cinq Colonnes à la Une.* Normally, of course, you do not say *la une* nor *le un*, but *l'une* and *l'un. Ils se regardaient l'un l'autre.* 'They looked at one another.' *De deux choses l'une.* 'One of two things is possible'. *L'une des deux sœurs est jolie.* 'One of the two sisters is pretty.'

un tel (or *Untel*). 'So-and-So'. *Supposez que vous rencontrez Madame Unetelle (Monsieur Untel).* 'Suppose you meet Mrs. So-and-So (Mr. So-and-So).'

V

valable. First of all, 'valid'. In the Métro: *Au-delà de cette limite, les billets ne sont plus valables.* 'All tickets are invalid beyond this line.' *Il n'a pas d'excuse valable.* 'He has no valid excuse.' Closely linked to another meaning, 'worthwhile'. *C'était une expérience valable.* 'It was a worthwhile experience' (or experiment: *v.* EXPÉRIENCE).

But this is not the way to translate 'valuable', which is *précieux* or *ayant beaucoup de valeur.* 'That eighteenth-century bust is very valuable.' *Ce buste dix-huitième est très précieux.*

Nor is it the word for 'valuables', which are more properly *des objets* (or *effets*) *personnels de valeur.*

valide. Can have the same meaning as *valable* but also, and especially, means 'sound': *les personnes valides*, as opposed to 'the crippled', *les invalides.* Yet the verb *valider* and its contrary, *invalider*, have nothing to do with health but rather with contracts, bills and tickets: 'to validate' and 'invalidate'.

verser. 'To pour a liquid'; also 'to pour money'—that is 'to pay'. 'A payment' can be called *un versement. Cette somme est à verser à la banque.* 'This sum is to be paid into the bank.'

Je paie ma voiture en neuf versements mensuels. 'I'm paying for my car in nine monthly instalments.' *Verser des arrhes*, 'to make a down payment'.

vignette (f). Among other things, a sort of car license—not the driver's license, which is *le permis de conduire*—which you have to renew every year around November. You buy it in a *bureau de tabac*, and its price varies according to the year and the horsepower of your car.

Or again, a minuscule tab of gummed paper, with or without the price marked, on the outside of any package of medicine whose cost is partly reimbursed to you by *la Sécurité Sociale*. You have to peel the *vignette* off the box and stick it onto the prescription, *l'ordonnance*, which you send in to the *Sécurité Sociale* along with a *feuille de maladie*, or doctor's certificate.

vin d'honneur (m). A reception to honor some person or group, or to mark an occasion, as the victory of one team over another, the arrival of a foreign delegation, and the like.

virgule (f). 'The comma' in a sentence, and 'the decimal point' in a number. Conversely, where English uses a comma in numbers—as to separate hundreds from thousands—French uses points: 23.987.654,01 (*vingt-trois millions neuf cent quatre-vingt-sept mille six cent cinquante-quatre virgule zéro un*).

visite (f). 'Visit'; and *rendre visite* is 'to visit', 'call upon' someone; whereas *visiter* applies mostly to edifices (*visiter les Invalides à Paris*) and countries. You cannot *rendre visite à un monument*; conversely, *visiter* is rarely used for persons except when they are looked at from an institutional point of view: *visiter des orphelins*.

Passer une visite médicale is 'to go through a medical examination'.

voir. You might add these expressions having to do with 'see' and 'see about' to those you will find in a dictionary:

Cela n'a rien à voir là-dedans (or *avec cela*): 'That has nothing to do with it, that's beside the point' (*v.* also RAPPORTER).

C'est tout vu, 'it's all decided', 'no argument'.

Il ne peut pas les voir en peinture. 'He can't stand them.'

Avant d'agir, je préfère attendre et voir venir. 'Before doing anything, I'd rather wait and see how things shape up.'

volontaire. Unites two ideas which English expresses in separate words: 'voluntary', and 'strong-willed' or 'stubborn'. *Il a le menton volontaire.* 'He has a stubborn chin.' *Un volontaire* is 'a volunteer'; *se porter volontaire*, 'to enlist' or 'volunteer'.

vue (f). 'Eyesight' or 'vision' (*v.* PRESBYTE). *Avoir une bonne vue*, 'to have good eyesight'. *Avoir la vue faible*, 'to have bad eyesight'. Also, 'a view', as in *cette maison a vue sur la mer.* 'This house has a view of the sea (overlooks the sea).'

Or 'sight' in general. *A la vue de tant de travail, il faillit s'évanouir.* 'He nearly fainted at the sight of so much work'.

Perdre quelqu'un de vue, 'to lose sight of someone', 'to lose track of *or* be out of touch with someone'.

A perte de vue: literally, 'out of sight', 'endlessly'.

Z

zinc (m). Another term for *le comptoir*, 'the counter', in a café. *Manger (boire) sur le zinc,* 'to eat (drink) standing up at the counter'.

SPECIAL VOCABULARIES

LA BANQUE

BANKING

Here are some of the more necessary items in a simplified everyday vocabulary:

action (f): 'stock-market share'.

barème (m): 'table', 'scale' (for calculating rates etc.).
billet (m): 'bank note' (US: 'bill').
bordereau (m): 'statement', 'paying-in receipt'.
Bourse (f): 'stock market', 'Exchange'.

caissier (m): 'cashier'.
carnet de chèques (m): 'checkbook'.
change (m): 'exchange of currencies', 'rate of exchange'.
chèque de voyage (m): 'traveller's check'.
coffre-fort (m): 'strongbox', 'safe'.
compte (m): an 'account'.
courtier (m): 'stockbroker', 'Exchange agent'.

encaisser: 'to cash' or 'collect' a check (from a bank's point of view).
endosser: 'to endorse' a check, like this:
   Pour acquit, à Paris, le 30 Juin 1966, Jean Dupont.

intérêts (m. pl.): 'interest'.

monnaie (f): 'change'. *Les monnaies étrangères*, 'foreign currencies'.

pièce (f): 'coin'.
placer (son argent): 'to invest one's money'; *placement* (m): 'investment'.
prélever (sur un compte): 'to deduct' (from an account); *prélèvement* (m): 'deduction'.

relevé (m) **trimestriel**, 'quarterly statement'.
retirer, 'to withdraw'.

somme (f), a 'sum'.
souche (f), 'stub'.

toucher (un chèque, une somme), 'to cash' a check (from your point of view).
traite (f), 'draft' (as, credit payment deducted directly from your account).
transfert (m), 'transfer'; *transférer*, 'to transfer'.

verser, 'to pay', 'to pay into an account'.

Banks are generally open from 9 a.m. to 4.30 p.m. (*de 9h à 16h30 sans interruption*), from Monday to Friday.

FAUX AMIS

FALSE FRIENDS

You will have noticed that every so often in the main text, we have accused certain words of being *des Faux Amis*, 'false friends'. A *Faux Ami* looks so much like a word in English that you are sure it means the same—and there you are headed straight for disaster in the form of *un contre-sens*, 'a nonsensical translation'; *une gaffe*, 'a blunder'; or *un malentendu*, 'a misunderstanding'.

Still other words are traitors only some of the time. *Accuser*, for instance, does mean 'to accuse'; it also, when referring not to people but to things, means 'to underline', 'stress': *des traits accusés*, 'sharp features'; *des jaunes accusés dans un tableau*, 'strong yellows in a painting'. And *accuser réception* (of a letter) is 'to acknowledge receipt'. The following list, including only some of the more recurrent or more bothersome cases, is perhaps dangerously succinct; you are advised to take it merely as an invitation to look into each case more thoroughly. Intransitive verbs are given with the appropriate prepositions.

accommoder: to accompany with a sauce.

accomplissement (m): achievement, completion.

actuel: present, current;
à l'heure actuelle: at the present moment;
les actualités: the news.

apologie (f): defense, praise;
faire l'apologie de quelqu'un: to praise someone.

application (f): the fact of applying something to something else.

apprécier: estimate.

argument (m): reason, justification.

assistance (f): audience, public (*also* assistance, aid, Welfare).

assister à: to attend.

accommodate: loger, caser, contenir.

accomplishment: talent (m), art (m).

actual: vrai, véridique, réel.

apology: excuses (f. pl.);
faire ses excuses à quelqu'un, s'excuser: **to apologize**.

application (request): demande (f).

appreciate: reconnaître la juste valeur de; **to be appreciative**: être reconnaissant.

argument: discussion (f), querelle (f).

assistance: aide (f), secours (m).

assist: aider, venir en aide à, porter secours à.

attendre: to wait.
axe (m): axis.

attend: assister à.
axe: hache (f).

box (m): garage.
boxe (f): boxing.
brigadier (m): corporal.

box: boîte (f).

brigadier general: général (m) de brigade.

caméra (f): motion-picture camera.
candide: gullible, credulous.
car (m): coach, bus.

camera: appareil (m) photo.

candid: franc.
car: voiture (f), automobile (f).
case (f): box, compartment; hut.
casque (m): helmet.
casquette (f): cap.

case: cas (m); procès (m); étui (m).
cask: tonneau (m).
casket: coffret (m); cercueil (m).
cave (f): cellar.
charte (f): charter.

cave: grotte (f), caverne (f).
chart: carte (f); graphique (m).
commodité (f): comfort, convenience.
conférence (f): lecture, speech.
confidence (f): secret;
　faire une confidence à: to confide in.
confusion (f); embarrassment; (*also* confusion).
　être confus: to be embarrassed
contenance (f): amount contained, capacity.
contrôle (m): checkup, surveillance;
　contrôler: to check on, verify.
courtier (m): broker, Exchange agent.

commodity: article (m) de consommation courante.
conference: congrès (m), réunion (f).
confidence: confiance (f); **to be confident**: avoir confiance, être confiant.
confusion: chaos (m), désordre (m);
　also confusion (f).

countenance: visage (m), figure (f).
control: direction (f), discipline (f);
　to control: guider, diriger, être maître de.
courtier: courtisan (m).

délai (m): time limit.
délayer: to dilute, stir in.
détenir (le pouvoir, la vérité etc.): to possess *or* keep.
disgracieux: awkward, graceless, ugly.

delay: retard (m).
delay: retarder.
detain: retarder, arrêter.

disgraceful: honteux.

entretenir: to maintain, keep (up).

entertain: amuser, divertir.

éventuel: possible, conceivable;
  éventualité (f): possibility.
  éventuellement: in the event of, if need be.
expérience (f): experiment; *also* experience;
  expérimenté: experienced.

eventual: final, définitif.

eventually: en définitive, finalement.
experience: aventure (f), expérience (f).

fabrique (f): factory.
faute (f): (moral) fault *or* blame;
  sans faute: without fail.
figure (f): face.

fabric: tissu (m), étoffe (f).
fault (*defect, flaw*): défaut (m).

figure (*shape*): ligne (f).
figure (*number*): chiffre (m).
fournitures (f. pl.): supplies.

furniture: mobilier (m).
  an item of furniture: meuble (m).

génial: ingenious, clever.
grappe (f): bunch (of grapes etc.).
gratuit: free, gratuitous.
grief (m): grievance, grudge.

groom (m): bellboy.

genial: sympathique.
grape: raisin (m).

gratuity: pourboire (m).
grief: douleur (f), chagrin (m).
groom (*bride*): marié (m).
groom (*stable boy*): garçon d'écuries (m).

habit (m): formal evening-wear.
habits (m.pl.): clothes.
hardi: bold.

habit: habitude (f).

hardy: robuste.

important: big; *also* important.
incessamment: very soon.
informations (f. pl.): news (*as on the radio or in the paper*).
inhabité: uninhabited.
injure (f): insult.
intoxication (f): poisoning.

important: significatif; *also* important.
unceasingly: sans arrêt.
information: renseignements (m. pl.).

inhabited: habité.
injury: blessure (f).
intoxication: ivresse (f).

large: wide.
lecture (f): reading.
limonade (f): lemon soda.
lunatique: fickle.

large: grand.
lecture: conférence (f).
lemonade: citron (m) pressé.
lunatic: fou (m).

malice (f): mischief.
  malicieux: mischievous.

malice: méchanceté (f);
  malicious: méchant.

nappe (f): table cloth.
nègre: (Negro) *is pejorative*.
nouvelle (f): short story;
  nouvelles (f. pl.): news
  (*being replaced today by*
  informations *and* **actualités**).

nap: somme (m).
Negro: Noir.
novel: roman (m).

office (f): pantry.

office: bureau (m).

pâte (f): dough.
pet (m): fart.
photographe (m): photographer.

paste (*glue*): colle (f).
pet: animal favori (m).
photograph: photographie (f).
  photography: photographie
  (f).

physicien (m): physicist.
pomme de pin (f): pine cone.
préjudice (m): a wrong done
  to someone.
prétendre: to claim, assert.

physician: médecin (m).
pineapple: ananas (m).
prejudice: préjugé (m), parti
  pris (m).
pretend (*make believe*): faire
  semblant de, faire mine
  de.

prune (f): plum.
pulvériser: to vaporize
  (liquid); *also* to pulverize.

prune: pruneau (m).
pulverize: écraser, réduire
  en poudre.

raisin (m): grape.
reste (m): remainder.
rester: to remain.
résumer: to summarize;
  résumé (m): summary.

raisin: raisin sec (m).
rest: repos (m).
rest: se reposer.
resume: reprendre, poursuivre.

sensible: sensitive; *also*
  marked, pronounced, *as*
  une hausse sensible.
store (m): awning, blind,
  shade.
supplier: beg, beseech.
sympathique: congenial, nice.

sensible: sensé, raisonnable.

store (*shop*): boutique (f),
  magasin (m).
supply: fournir, ravitailler.
sympathetic: compatissant.

trouble (m): disturbance,
  anxiety;
  troubler: to disturb, make
  uneasy;
  eau trouble: unclear water.

trouble: ennui (m), difficulté
  (f), du mal (avoir).

usage (m): custom;
  usager (m): user (of public
  transport).
user: to wear out.

usage: emploi (m).

use: se servir de, employer.

versatile: unstable, fickle, unreliable.	**versatile**: ayant de multiples dons, ayant plusieurs cordes à son arc.
voyage (m): any sort of trip; **voyageur** (m): traveller.	**voyage** (i.e. *sea trip*): traversée (f), voyage (m) par mer.
wagon (m): car, coach (of train).	**wagon**: charrette (f).

FORMULES DE POLITESSE

COURTESY

It is an old story that French is the language of politeness, and even today, the outward forms, the standard phrases have been preserved to a far greater extent than in English. You must learn them off pat and be able to handle them with assurance. This makes it sound as though they are necessarily hypocritical; they are not. They are simply built in; and without them, the average conversation, introduction or—especially—letter would fall apart.

In the Paris Métro, for instance, a sign will tell you that you may not go down onto the tracks *à moins d'y avoir été expressément invité par les agents de la R.A.T.P.*: 'unless you have been expressly invited by representatives of the *Régie Autonome des Transports Parisiens*'. The use of *inviter* is quite unexpected to the English-speaking person. And where in English you would say 'Please go out through this door', the Frenchman will say *Mesdames et Messieurs, vous êtes priés de bien vouloir sortir par ici.*

The imperative is frequently eschewed and the infinitive used instead. When you send photographs through the mail, you mark on the envelope 'Do not bend'. The Frenchman will write *Ne pas plier.*

To say of someone that he is polite, you say either that he is *poli*, or that he is wellbred: *Il est bien élevé*; or *Il a une bonne éducation*. The opposite is *impoli* or, more frequently, *mal élevé*; or again, *il manque d'éducation.*

An indication of the relative formality of French courtesy is that the *carte de visite*—visiting card—is very commonly used for communication between friends, even very young ones and even on a modest social level. This is also the standard way of sending New Year's wishes; and you have the entire month of January to get around to doing so.

A sample conversation might begin like this:

Monsieur Lebrun, permettez-moi de vous présenter (je vous présente) Madame Leblanc. 'Mr. Lebrun, allow me to introduce Mrs. Leblanc.'

Enchanté, Madame (de faire votre connaissance). Comment allez-vous? 'Pleased to meet you, Mrs. Leblanc. How are you?'

Très bien, Monsieur, je vous remercie. Et vous-même? 'Fine, thank you; and you?'

And on saying goodbye, let us suppose that Monsieur Lebrun has done Madame Leblanc a favor or service of some sort:

Vous êtes vraiment trop aimable, Monsieur, je suis confuse. Merci mille fois (or tous mes remerciements). 'It's really too kind of you, Mr. Lebrun; I'm most embarrassed. Thank you ever so much.'

Mais, je vous en prie (or il n'y a pas de quoi), c'est tout naturel. (More colloquially, Mr. Lebrun could say *de rien*: 'not at all', 'it's nothing really'.)

Au revoir, Monsieur. 'Goodbye, Mr. Lebrun.'

Au revoir, Madame, je suis très content d'avoir fait votre connaissance. 'Goodbye, Mrs. Leblanc. I'm delighted to have met you.'

When you step back to let someone go through a doorway or down the stairs before you, you say simply *Passez, Madame (Mademoiselle, Monsieur), je vous en prie.* You may also hear, in this connection, *faites*, or *faites donc*: literally, 'do'; in other words, 'go ahead'.

On entering or leaving a shop in which other customers are already waiting, you are expected to mutter *Messieurs dames.* Well-meaning people will tell you that this is not really a proper form of address, but you never hear any other. The shopkeeper will punctuate your transactions with a sort of singsong: *Bonjour, Madame. (Qu'est-ce que) vous désirez, Madame? Voici, Madame. Merci, Madame. Au revoir, Madame.*

In conversation, when you are on the verge of asking a prying question (*Combien gagne-t-il? Combien l'avez-vous payé? Vont-ils divorcer?* 'How much does he earn?' 'What did you pay for it?' 'Are they getting divorced?'), you excuse yourself in advance: *Je ne voudrais pas être indiscret, mais . . .* or, *sans indiscrétion . . .*, which authorizes you to go right ahead and pry.

The equivalent of 'God bless you!' when someone sneezes is *à vos (tes) souhaits!*

When you haven't been able to hear what someone said, you have, of course, a whole gamut of expressions, ranging from 'I beg your pardon?' down to 'what?' and 'huh?' *Je vous demande pardon? Pardon? Je m'excuse? Vous dites? (Tu dis?).* Or simply *Comment?* But you need to be careful of *comment*; everything depends on the tone of voice. You can make it inquire, be indignant (like *ah mais!* or *ça alors!*), scold, joke, or merely express surprise.

When you must ask someone to keep quiet, courtesy requires *un peu de silence, s'il vous plaît*, or *un instant, je vous prie*, or *veuillez m'écouter. Taisez-vous (tais-toi)* is obviously much more abrupt, much less polite, and can be used only with more intimate acquaintances or children: 'keep quiet'. *Fermez-la* or *bouclez-la!* is definitely rude: 'shut up'.

The writing of a business letter is a particularly delicate and subtle matter. There are more gradations of esteem and familiarity than in English, where you have little choice outside 'Dear Mr. Smith' or 'Dear John'.

In French, at the stage of greatest remoteness, or respect, you start with *Monsieur* (or *Madame* or *Mademoiselle*) on a line by itself, never abbreviated, usually near the center of the page instead of being towards the upper left, and followed by a comma. Only very gradually, and perhaps never, will you work up to *Cher Monsieur* (*Chère Madame* or *Mademoiselle*); then, rarely to *Cher Ami* (*Chère Amie*); and the ultimate in intimacy would be *Mon cher ami* (*Ma chère amie*) or *Mon cher Jean* (*Ma chère Jeanne*). If you are addressing someone with a professional title, as Minister, Doctor, Professor, then you start with *Monsieur le Ministre* (*le Docteur, le Professeur*).

The mode of address which you have used at the beginning will be repeated in the closing of your letter, a much more elaborate affair than in present-day English, which contents itself with 'Best wishes. Yours truly,'. The variety of *formules* from which you may, and must, choose in French will remind you of the 'I beg you, Madame, to believe me your most humble and obedient servant,' which unhappily disappeared long ago from English usage.

Croyez, chère Madame, à l'expression, or *Veuillez agréer, chère Madame, l'expression de mes sentiments distingués (dévoués, les meilleurs)* is the most frequently found form of closing. *Croyez . . . à,* and *Veuillez agréer* are of course a little more peremptory than *Je vous prie de croire à* (or *d'agréer, d'accepter) l'assurance* (or *l'expression) de mes sentiments distingués* etc. And if you are writing to someone who is distinctly your superior or from whom you are asking a favor, you might use . . . *mes sentiments respectueux.*

If writing to an official for some permission or other, you may start out after the salutation *J'ai l'honneur de solliciter de votre haute bienveillance la permission de . . .*

If you are writing to acknowledge a letter, *J'ai l'honneur d'accuser réception de votre lettre du 16 courant* ('I am pleased to acknowledge receipt of yours of the 16th instant'); or more simply, *Je vous remercie de votre lettre . . .*

If you are requesting an appointment with someone you do not know, you might say *Seriez-vous assez aimable pour m'accorder un rendez-vous,* or *Je vous serais reconnaissant de bien vouloir m'accorder* etc. If, however, you are writing to someone whom you do know reasonably well, you could use *Ayez la bonté (l'amabilité) de m'accorder* etc. Or more familiarly still, *Vous serez bien gentil de . . .* A polite command would be *Vous voudrez bien (me téléphoner, me dire ce qu'il en est,* etc.).

FRANGLAIS

Much has been said and written about, mostly against, the relatively recent phenomenon called *le Franglais*: the introduction, willy-nilly, of English words into French where, often, there is no need for them or where they are incorrectly adapted.[1] We will by no means attempt to give you a complete lexicon of *Franglais*. For a very comprehensive and critical study of it, we can recommend *Parlez-vous Franglais?* by Etiemble, Gallimard ('Idées'), Paris, 1964. We will simply say that things will probably get worse before they get better, so that a hundred years from now, perhaps, students of philology on both sides of the Channel and of the Atlantic will pore over Old and Middle Franglais. . . .

But here is a sample, at least of the more striking cases:

auto-stop (m): 'hitchhiking'.
auto-stoppeur (m): 'hitchhiker'.
biftek (m): '(beef)steak', instead of *la tranche de bœuf*.
building (m): *un immeuble, un édifice*.
cardigan (m): 'cardigan', instead of *le gilet*.
footing (m): *la marche à pied*.
job (m): 'job', instead of *la situation*.
meeting (m): *une réunion, une rencontre*.
pull(-over) (m): 'jumper' (US: sweater), instead of *le tricot*; *pull-over* is pronounced '*pule-ovaire*'.
relaxe (m): 'relaxation', instead of *la détente, le repos*. Also **se relaxer**, meaning *se détendre*.
shake-hand (m) 'handshake', instead of *la poignée de main*.
snack (m): 'snack bar'.
waters (m. pl.): 'lavatory', instead of *les cabinets*.
weekend (m): 'weekend', instead of *la fin de semaine*. You virtually never hear *Bonne fin de semaine!* any more, and only at times *Bon dimanche!* They are superseded by *Bon weekend!*

In the fields of cosmetics and clothing, examples are everywhere you look. There seems to be a special penchant for English words ending in '-ing.' The most notable of all is probably **le standing**, meaning *le prestige*. *Un immeuble de très grand standing*, 'a very prestigious *or* high-class building'. A not quite accurate transplantation.

Le living is another case in point, since in English the full term is 'the living room', and since French already possesses a couple of perfectly adequate words: *le salon*, or *la salle de séjour*. But

---

[1] It does not follow, however, that you can invent words in French with impunity as you can with relative ease in English. In general, the French have a more conservative attitude to the non-Franglais bulk of their language and the foreigner who bravely invents a new word will, nine times out of ten, be squelched: *Non, ça ne se dit pas.*

'*le living*' *fait plus jeune, plus à la page:* '*le living*' sounds more modern and up to date'.

Le smoking is a notorious *Faux Ami*. As it has been absorbed into French, the word means 'a tuxedo' or 'dinner jacket'.

Le shopping replaces *les achats: faire du shopping, faire des achats, aller dans les magasins.* '*Le shopping*' *est plus* '*snob*'—and **snob** itself is a good instance of Franglais, since it is used where in English you would say 'snobbish' or 'fashionable, and is pronounced *snub*.

And so on and on. **Le pressing** means *la teinturerie* ('cleaners and dyers'), and has nothing to do with either *être pressé* ('to be in a hurry') or *la presse* ('the press', 'journalism').

Le Franglais also comes into its own in the vast world of sports: **le basket**, 'basketball'; **le rugby**; **le soccer** (pronounced *socaire*); **un match**.

LE GENRE

GENDERS

Here are some instances of genders which may surprise you because the end of the word 'looks as though' it should belong to the opposite gender, or because the very meaning of the word would seem to place it in the opposite camp—as in the case of *barbe* and *moustache*. You know, of course, that the same thing can sometimes be designated by two or more words of different genders. The face, for instance, is either *le visage* or *la figure*.

Surprising genders:

masculine	*feminine*
caprice: whim.	**barbe**: beard.
espace: space.	**cuisson**: cooking.
génie: genius.	**dactylo**: typist.
incendie: fire.	**faux**: scythe.
manque: lack.	**fourmi**: ant.
musée: museum.	**moustache**: moustache.
pamplemousse: grapefruit.	**radio**: radio, X-ray.
parapluie: umbrella.	**toux**: cough.
reproche: reproach.	
scarabée: beetle.	
site: landscape.	
squelette: skeleton.	

And there are three celebrated words which, although masculine in the singular, are feminine in the plural:

amour: *un bel amour; de belles amours*[1]

[1] Note, however, that *un amour* when it means 'a cherub' remains masculine in the plural.

délice: *un tel délice; de telles délices*
orgue: *un grand orgue; de grandes orgues*

Double genders:

le box: garage.
le critique: critic.
le livre: book.
le manche: handle.

la boxe: boxing.
la critique: criticism.
la livre: pound.
la manche: sleeve; half (of game);
la Manche, English Channel; also a *département* in Normandy.

le mode: directions for use; mood (*grammar*).
le poêle: stove, furnace; pall.
le poste: job; radio *or* TV set.
le solde: clearance sale; balance to pay.
le somme: nap.
le tour: a walk (around); trick.
le vase: vase.
le voile: veil.

la mode: fashion, manner.
la poêle: frying pan.
la poste: mail, post office.

la solde: soldier's pay.

la somme: sum.
la tour: tower.

la vase: mud.
la voile: sail.

L'HEURE

TELLING THE TIME

Avez-vous l'heure (exacte), s'il vous plaît? 'Can you tell me (exactly) what time it is, please?'
Ma montre avance: 'my watch is fast'.
Ma montre retarde (or **a du retard**): 'my watch is slow'.
Il est dix heures trente.
Il est dix heures et demie: } 'It's half past ten' (a.m. or p.m.).
Il est vingt-deux heures trente: 'It's half past ten p.m.' *You do not* say *vingt-deux heures et demie.*
Il est moins cinq: 'It's five (minutes) to', 'of'.
Il est moins le quart: 'It's a quarter to', 'of'.
Il est le quart: 'It's a quarter past, after'.
Il est la demie: 'It's half past, after'.
Il est l'heure: 'It's time' (to leave, eat, get ready, etc.).
Huit jours (une huitaine): by far the most common way of saying 'a week'. *J'attends sa réponse sous huitaine*: 'I expect his answer within a week.'

Quinze jours (une quinzaine): similarly, for 'two weeks', 'a fort-night'. *Il a remis sa visite à une quinzaine de jours*: 'He's put off his visit for a fortnight'.

En huit: 'a week from' . . . *Mardi en huit*: 'a week from Tuesday'.

En quinze: 'two weeks from' . . . *Mardi en quinze*: 'two weeks from Tuesday'.

D'ici trois jours (deux mois etc.): 'Three days (two months) from now'.

Il y a dix jours: 'ten days ago'. *Elle est partie il y a un an hier*: 'She left a year ago yesterday'.

Il était (or Il y avait) une fois: 'Once upon a time . . .'

Tous les combien? 'How often?'

Tous les six mois: 'every six months'.

Toutes les trois minutes: 'every three minutes'.

Tous les deux jours: 'every other day'.

Tous les 16 du mois: 'every month on the 16th'.

Tous les midis: 'every noon'.

Tous les deux: 'both'.

Cette nuit ('this night') is the continuation of **ce soir** ('this even-ing'); in other words, 'tonight'.

La nuit dernière is the continuation of **hier soir** ('yesterday evening'); in other words, 'last night'. *J'ai eu (or fait) des cauchemars la nuit dernière*. 'I had nightmares last night'.

Demain soir, 'tomorrow evening', 'tomorrow night'.

A bientôt: 'So long', 'I'll see you soon'.

A ce soir: 'Till this evening'.

A demain: 'Till tomorrow'.

A (tout) jamais: 'For ever'.

Jamais: 'Ever'. *Si jamais vous venez. . . .* 'If you ever come. . . .'

Ne . . . jamais: 'Never'. *Ne venez jamais.* 'Never come'.

Jamais (de la vie)!: 'Never!' 'Not on your life!'

Jamais, au grand jamais!: 'Never!'

Plus jamais!: 'Never again!'

A l'instant: 'A minute ago', 'just now'. *Je l'ai vu à l'instant*.

A la prochaine: 'Till I see you again'. This is rather *familier*.

A tantôt, or **A cet après-midi**: 'Till this afternoon.' In certain provinces you can hear *je l'ai vu hier tantôt*: 'I saw him yesterday afternoon'.

Au début de la soirée: 'late in the afternoon', 'early in the evening'.

A tout à l'heure: 'I'll see you later' (in a very short while).

A tout de suite: 'I'll see you (be back) in a minute'.

LES NUMÉROS

NUMBERS

Certain numbers keep recurring in idiomatic French; the most obvious example is probably thirty-six: a loose way of indicating 'a lot', 'a thousand and one', 'hundreds', and the like.

Il n'y a pas trente-six façons de s'y prendre: 'There's only one way of going about it.'

Elle a toujours 36 projets en tête: 'She's always got a dozen different plans.'

En voir 36 chandelles: 'to be knocked out', 'to see stars'.

The number 'four' also crops up quite often as a vague indication of 'several', 'more than one'.

Quand il a quelque chose à dire, il n'y va pas par quatre chemins. 'When he's got something he wants to say, he doesn't beat around the bush.'

Faire ses quatre volontés: 'to do whatever one likes' (and, the implication is, 'to get away with it').

Etre tiré à quatre épingles: 'to be dressed to the nines' ('down to the last detail').

Couper les cheveux en quatre: 'to split hairs'.

Un quatre heures (*v.* GOÛTER): 'afternoon tea *or* snack'.

Etre à deux doigts de faire quelque chose: 'to be on the verge of doing something'. *Il était à deux doigts de tout plaquer*: 'He came very close to dropping the whole business.'

Trois fois rien: 'less than nothing', 'dirt cheap' etc. *Ils l'ont payé trois fois rien:* 'They got it for next to nothing.'

Faire quelque chose en trois (or sometimes, **deux**) **temps trois mouvements**: 'to do something in the twinkling of an eye', 'before you can say Jack Robinson'.

En cinq sept: *à toute vitesse*, 'quick as lightning'.

Se mettre sur son trente-et-un: *s'endimancher*, 'to wear one's Sunday best'.

Passer un mauvais quart d'heure (or **un mauvais moment**): 'to have a bad time of it'. *J'ai passé un mauvais quart d'heure chez le dentiste.*

In talking about a decade—'the Forties', 'the Twenties'—you simply say *les années* and then add the cardinal number: *les années 40, les années 20.*

LANGAGE FAMILIER

FAMILIAR, OR INFORMAL, FRENCH

This is not necessarily vulgar language, except for rare instances, which we have pointed out as such. No; the following are a small portion of the great number of expressions which are spoken and heard far more often than they are written and read. Nor are they slang, since, as explained in the Introduction, we have in no way aimed at listing or translating *des expressions argotiques*. You can get by very well without using any of the terms of this small sampling of *langage familier*, and in fact it might be better if you did not try to use it. None the less, you will frequently need to understand it—in conversation, in novels, and at the cinema.

It may be wise to remember that the degree of familiarity or even vulgarity of a given expression depends largely on (*a*) who is saying it, (*b*) to whom, (*c*) how, and (*d*) in what circumstances.

attraper: 'to scold', 'tell off' (*v. engueuler*).

bagnole (f): 'car', 'automobile'.
bain (m): *être dans le bain* (or *le coup*): 'to be involved'; also 'to be in the know'.
balle (f): *le franc ancien. J'ai mille balles.* 'I have 1,000 old francs (10 new francs).'
bidule (m): 'thing'. Even more colloquial than *machin* and *truc*.
billet (m): '10 new francs'. Also called *un ticket. Ça m'a coûté 100 billets (100 tickets).* For the more general meaning of *billet* *v.* the chapter on LA BANQUE.
blague (f): 'nonsense', 'sham', 'fake'. *C'est de la blague! Blague à part, blague dans le coin, sans blague!* 'no joke!' 'for real!'
blagueur (m): 'joker', 'faker'.
bled (m) (adapted from the Arabic) 'an out-of-the-way hamlet', 'one-horse town', *v.* also *patelin, trou.*
bosser: *travailler*, 'to work'; *v.* also *trimer.*
bouffe (f): 'food'. **Bouffer:** 'to grub'. Inelegant.
boulot (m): 'work'.
bousiller: 'to ruin', 'damage', 'put out of joint'. *Sa voiture est bousillée.* 'His car's all ruined'.
boustifaille (f): 'food', 'grub'. **Boustifailler:** 'to grub'. More vulgar than *bouffer.*

cancre (m): 'dunce'.
casser: *Ça ne casse rien!* 'it's no great shakes', 'nothing to write home about'. *Ça ne casse pas des briques* is a still more *familier* way of saying this. *Casser sa pipe*: 'mourir'. *Le casse-pipe*: 'war' (from the time of the Napoleonic wars when a wounded man,

operated on without anaesthetic, was given a pipe to bite on).
Casser les pieds à quelqu'un, 'to give someone a pain in the neck'.
Also *être casse-pieds*, 'to be a real pest'.

chic: 'nice', 'generous'. *Un chic type*, 'a good chap' (*v. type*).

chic (m): 'flair', 'gift', 'smartness'.

chouette: 'great', 'fine'. *C'était chouette*. 'It was just great.' Said
with ironic intention, it can mean just the opposite.

cochon: 'dirty', 'lewd'. *Une histoire cochonne*, 'a dirty story'.

coller: 'to stand up', 'be plausible'. *Son histoire ne colle pas*. 'His
story won't wash.' Like *son histoire ne tient pas debout*.

copain (m), **copine** (f): 'pal', 'buddy'. More correctly, *camarade*
(m. *or* f.).

cosse (f): 'laziness'. *Avoir la cosse; être cossard*.

costaud: 'strong', 'sturdy', 'resistant' (person, cloth, object).

coton: *C'est coton* means *C'est difficile. C'était drôlement coton!* 'It
was awfully hard.'

couci-couça: means *comme ci.comme ça*: 'so-so'.

cra cra: means *crasseux*: 'filthy'. (*La crasse*: 'filth'.)

croque-mort (m): 'undertaker'. Rather pejorative. More
properly: *un employé des pompes funèbres*.

culot (m): 'nerve', 'cheek', 'gall'. Like *toupet* (m). *Etre culotté*,
'to have a lot of cheek', 'have some nerve'.

cuit: *C'est cuit*: 'it's all up', 'finished', 'no good'; like *c'est fichu*.
Also, *je suis cuit, je suis fichu, je suis de la revue*: 'it's all up with
me'. Also, *les carottes sont cuites*.

cuite (f): 'drinking spree'. *Prendre une cuite*: 'to get soaked,
drunk'.

déveine (f): 'bad luck'. *C'est la déveine*. 'That's tough luck' (*v.
veine*).

encaisser: means *supporter*, 'to stand' or 'bear'. *Je ne peux pas
l'encaisser*. 'I can't stand him' (*v. also peinture, sentir*). Also
means *recevoir des coups*, 'to put up with'. *Qu'est-ce qu'il a fallu
encaisser!*

engueuler: 'to bawl out', 'give someone what for'. *Une engueulade*,
'a dressing-down'.

fabriquer: 'to do', 'be up to' (something). *Qu'est-ce que tu fa-
briques?* 'What are you doing?'

fauché: 'broke', 'penniless'. Also *être raide, être sans un*.

flic (m): 'bobby', 'cop'. Also, more slangily, *une hirondelle, un
poulet*.

flopée, floppée (f): 'a whole lot', 'a flock', 'a swarm' (of people or
things); perhaps a less desirable word than *ribambelle* (f).

foutre. Vigorously *incorrect*—i.e. 'bad' language. Expressions
like *je m'en fous* ('I don't give a damn'), *sa foutue idée, c'est foutu*
('it's shot', 'it's all up', 'ruined' etc.) can, and had better, be
replaced by *fiche* and *fichu; je m'en fiche, sa fichue idée, c'est
fichu*. . . .

frais-frais: certain adjectives can be used in repetition like this in a negative sentence. *Ce vin n'est pas frais-frais.* 'This wine is not very cool.' *Il n'est pas riche-riche.* 'He's not very rich.'

fric (m): 'money', 'dough'. Also *la galette.*

frousse (f): *Avoir la frousse*, 'to be scared stiff'. Also, *avoir une frousse bleue.* A vulgar way of saying it is *avoir la trouille.*

fusiller: *Se faire fusiller* means, properly speaking, 'to be shot by a firing squad'; figuratively, *se faire engueuler*, i.e. 'to get a good dressing down'.

gonflé, être: 'to have a lot of nerve'.

gosse (m. or f.): 'kid, ' 'child', 'brat'. Can be said affectionately; much more frequent and generally acceptable than *môme* and *mioche.*

gougnaffier (m): 'careless (slob)', 'ignoramus'.

goujat (m): 'lout', 'boor'.

goupiller: 'to fix', 'arrange', 'set up something'. *Se goupiller*: 'to work'. *Comment ça se goupille?* 'How does that work?'

gris, être: 'to be tight, drunk'; v. also: *cuite, parti, rond.*

gueule (f): 'face', 'mug'. Definitely impolite when applied to a person. *Avoir la gueule de bois* (*G.D.B.*), 'to be hung over', 'to have a hangover'. *Les gueules noires*, 'coal miners'. *Les gueules cassées*, 'disfigured veterans'. *Gueuler*, 'to holler'; also 'to complain'. Rather vulgar. *Avoir de la gueule*, however, is complimentary: 'to be stunning'. *Ce dessin a de la gueule.*

guigne (f): 'bad luck'. More *familier* than *malchance* (f) and *déveine* (f); v. also *poisse.*

guigner: 'to covet something'.

lambiner: 'to dawdle'.

lapin (m): *Poser un lapin à quelqu'un*, 'to stand someone up'.

légume, une grosse: 'a big wig', 'big shot'. Note gender.

lessivé, être: 'to be dead', 'beat', 'dead tired'. Also *être vanné.*

magistral: 'enormous', 'thorough'. *Il a pris une cuite magistrale.* 'He got terribly tight.' *Elle est arrivée avec un retard magistral.* 'She arrived incredibly late.'

manigancer: 'to plot', 'intrigue'; like *combiner.* The noun is *la manigance.*

maous(se) or **mahous(se)**: 'enormous', 'gigantic'.

marrant: 'funny', 'comical'. *Se marrer*: 'to laugh'. *Qu'est-ce qu'on a pu se marrer!* 'How we laughed!'

marre, en avoir: 'to be fed up', 'be sick of something'; also, *il y en a marre, en avoir plein le dos, en avoir par dessus la tête.*

mec (m): 'chap', 'bloke'. Much slangier and shadier than *type* (q.v.).

minable: 'lousy', 'shabby', 'stunted'. Rather like *moche*; but you can also use *minable* as a noun when speaking of a person—*un petit minable.*

mirobolant: means *merveilleux, prestigieux.* Often encountered in the negative—*ce n'est pas une situation mirobolante*, 'that job's nothing special'.

moche: 'shabby', 'dowdy', 'dingy', 'ugly' (said of a person, room, object); 'lousy' (situation). Very common.

monstre: 'enormous', 'mammoth'. *Soldes monstres*, 'mammoth sales'.

mouise (f): *être dans la mouise*, 'to be flat broke'; like *être dans la panade* or, more correctly, *la misère*.

numéro (m): 'chap', 'guy', 'character'. *C'est un drôle de numéro.* 'He's a funny chap, a real character.'

oust!: 'scram!' 'scat!' 'get!'

paperasse (f): 'old paper(s)', 'waste paper'; by extension, 'bureaucratic waste', 'red tape'. *La paperasserie*, 'red tape'. Very common expression.

par exemple!: like *ça alors! ce n'est pas vrai!* Expresses scepticism or astonishment. Very common and innocuous.

parti: 'drunk'; *v. gris, rond* .

patelin (m): 'village'.

payer: *se payer la tête de quelqu'un*, 'to make fun of someone'.

pègre (f): 'the underworld'; from *la haute pègre—les gangsters, les souteneurs*—to *la basse pègre*, 'petty thieves' and 'pickpockets'.

peinture (f): *ne pas pouvoir voir quelqu'un en peinture*, 'to find someone unbearable'; *v.* also *encaisser, sentir*.

pépin (m): *avoir des pépins*, 'to be in trouble', 'have problems'. More properly, *avoir des ennuis*.

picrate (m): bad cheap wine.

pif (m): 'nose'. *Faire quelque chose au pif*, 'to do something *au hasard*, by instinct,' 'to follow one's nose'.

piger: 'to get it', 'to understand'. *Tu piges?* 'You get it?'

pinard (m): 'wine'.

plaquer: means *abandonner, quitter. Il a plaqué sa femme.* 'He's left his wife'.

poil, être à: 'to be naked'. Vulgar.

poil, être au: 'to be great , perfect'.

poire (f): means *imbécile*.

poireauter (or *poiroter*, or *faire le poireau*): 'to wait', or 'to be kept waiting'. *Faire poireauter quelqu'un.*

poisse (f): 'lousy luck'. *C'est la poisse.* Rather vulgar, and stronger than *déveine* (q.v.).

rasoir: 'boring', 'a bore'. *Se raser*, 'to get (be) bored'.

rigolade (f): 'fun', 'amusement'. But *c'est de la rigolade* means either 'it's nothing to be taken seriously' or 'it's easy to do'.

rigoler: 'to laugh', 'have fun'. *Je l'ai fait pour rigoler.* 'I did it just for kicks.'

riquiqui: 'skimpy', 'flimsy', 'undersized'.

rond, être: 'to be tight', 'drunk'; *v. gris, parti*. More correctly, *être ivre*.

rond (m): *ne pas avoir un rond*, 'to be stone broke'; *v.* also *fauché*.

sale: 'dirty', 'dirty little', 'lousy', 'nasty'. *C'est une sale histoire.* 'It's a nasty (*or* sordid) business.' ('A dirty story' is *une histoire cochonne, grivoise,* or *incorrecte,* or *un récit salé, osé.*) *Etre dans de sales* (or *beaux*) *draps* is a very strong way of saying 'to have got oneself into a real mess'.

sentir: *je ne peux pas la sentir,* 'I can't stand her' (*v.* also *encaisser, peinture*).

sorcier: *ce n'est pas sorcier,* 'there's nothing complicated about it', 'it's simple enough'.

tailler, se: 'to cut and run', 'run away'.

tonnerre (m): *c'est du tonnerre!* Means *c'est formidable,* or *épatant,* 'terrific'. *Une fille du tonnerre,* 'a very pretty girl', 'terrific looker'.

toubib (m): 'doctor'.

trimer: 'to work'; *v.* also *bosser*.

trou (m): 'hole', 'godforsaken town' (*v.* also *bled*).

type (m): 'chap', 'guy', 'fellow'. *Un brave type,* 'a good fellow'.

vache (f): *Ah la vache!* expresses reaction to a mean trick, a bad surprise, a nasty person. *Une vacherie* is 'a mean trick'. *Vachement,* however, is a strong, more vulgar version of *rudement, drôlement, bigrement*: *c'était vachement bien.*

veine (f): 'luck', 'good luck'. *Pas de veine,* 'bad luck'. *Un veinard,* 'lucky fellow'. Very common and innocuous (*v.* also *déveine*).

LE LOGEMENT

HOUSING

One of the topics which crop up most frequently in newspapers and conversation is the housing situation.

appartement (m): 'a flat', 'apartment'.

bail (m): 'lease'. The plural is *baux*.

chambre de bonne (f): 'maid's room', generally just under the eaves.

charges (f. pl.): 'periodic payments to *le syndic*' (q.v.).

confort (m): 'conveniences' (hot and cold running water, bathroom, heating etc.).

grand standing: 'prestige', 'luxury', 'high class' (*v.* the chapter on FRANGLAIS).

HLM: *Habitation* (f) *à Loyer Modéré* ('low-rent housing development').
immeuble (m) **en co-propriété**: 'building in which each flat is owned by the occupant'; a very common system. *Co-propriétaire* (m): owner of such a flat.

locataire (m. or f.): 'lodger', 'tenant'. *Sous-locataire*, lodger to whom one sublets.
louer: 'to let *or* rent'. *Louer à quelqu'un, sous-louer à quelqu'un*: 'to let to someone', 'to sublet'. *En location*: 'renting', 'rented', 'letting', 'let'.
loyer (m). 'rent'.

m²: *mètres carrés*, 'square meters' (measurement of floor surface).
meublé: 'furnished'.

non meublé: 'unfurnished'.

pavillon (m): 'house'.
pièce (f): 'room'.
pierre de taille (f): 'hewn stone'.

ravalement (m): 'repair and cleaning, *or* painting, of outside walls', now compulsory in Paris.
reprise (f): 'key money'; a lump sum which an incoming tenant must often pay to the old tenant for improvements made etc.

studio (m): 'one-room flat', 'bed-sitting-room'.
syndic (m): 'superintendent' charged with executing collective decisions of *co-propriétaires* as to repairs or insurance, for example.

villa (f): 'house', 'cottage'.

With this skeleton vocabulary in mind, you should find it easier to decipher the *petites annonces* (classified advertisements):

4/5 pp: four or five rooms.
s d'eau (or **s bns**): *salle de bains*, bathroom.
pet. c. (or **ktchntte**): small kitchen.
imm. g. stdg.: high-class building.
moquette: carpeting.
p de t: stone.
entr.: entry hall, vestibule.
s. à m.: dining room.
gr. séjour, gr. living: large living room.
asc.: lift (US: elevator).

ch. cent. indiv.: individual central heating.
tphne: telephone.
gd cft, tt cft: all conveniences.
vue imprenable: splendid view.
libre de suite: available for immediate occupancy.

LE MÉNAGE

THE HOUSEHOLD

accoudoir (m): arm of furniture.
aiguille (f): needle.
aiguille à tricoter (f): knitting needle.
alèze (f): rubber sheet.
argenterie (f): plate, silver.
armoire (f): wardrobe, closet.
armoire (f) **à médicaments**: ⎫
armoire (f) **à pharmacie**: ⎬ medicine cabinet.
aspirateur (m): vacuum cleaner.
assiette (f): plate, dish.
attrape-plats (m): pot holder.

bac (m): basin, vat.
bahut (m): long low cabinet, sideboard.
baignoire (f): bathtub.
balai (m): broom.
bassine (f): basin, pan.
batteur (m) **à œufs**: eggbeater.
berceau (m): cradle.
bidet (m): bidet.
bobine (f): spool of thread.
bol (m): bowl.
bouchon (m): bottle cap *or* stopper, cork.
bouilloire (f): kettle.
brosse (f): brush.
brûleur (m): burner *or* ring of stove.

canapé (m): sofa, couch.
carreau (m): window pane; tile.
carrelage (m): tiling.
casserole (f): pot, pan.
chaise (f): chair.
cheminée (f): fireplace; mantelpiece; chimney.
chiffon (m): rag, cloth.
chope (f): mug.

ciseau (m): chisel.
ciseaux (m. pl.): scissors.
clou (m): nail.
commode (f): commode, chest of drawers, dresser.
corbeille (f) **à papiers**: wastepaper basket.
coussin (m): cushion.
couvercle (m): lid.
couvert (m): place setting.
couverture (f): blanket.
couvre-lit (m): light bedspread.
crochet (m): hook.
cruche (f): pitcher.
cuisinière (f): stove; cook.
cuvette (f): (wash)basin.

dé (m): thimble.
dessus de lit (m): bedspread.
divan (m): couch, divan.
dossier (m): back of chair etc.
drap (m): sheet.

échelle (f): ladder.
écumoire (f): skimmer.
édredon (m): eiderdown.
épingle (f): pin.
épingle (f) **de sûreté:** ⎫
épingle (f) **de nourrice:** ⎬ safety pin.
escabeau (m): stepladder.
évier (m): kitchen sink.

fauteuil (m): armchair.
fenêtre (f): window.
fer à repasser (m): iron.
ficelle (f): string.
fil (m): thread.
four (m): oven.
fourneau (m): stove, furnace.

glace (f): looking glass.
guéridon (m): small round table.

housse (f): slipcover.

jeannette (f): sleeve ironing board.

laine (f): yarn, wool.
lavabo (m): washstand, sink.
lit (m): bed.
louche (f): ladle.

machine à coudre (f): sewing machine.
machine à laver (f): washing machine.
manche (m): handle.
marteau (m): hammer.
matelas (m): mattress.
meuble (m): piece of furniture.
miroir (m): mirror.
mobilier (m): furniture as a whole.
mur (m): wall.

nappe (f): tablecloth.
napperon (m): place mat.

oreiller (m): pillow.
ouvre-boîte (m): can opener.

panier à salade (m): salad shaker.
parquet (m): wood floor.
passoire (f): strainer.
pelle (f): shovel; dustpan.
pelote (f): ball (of string, yarn).
petit lit (m): crib.
pichet (m): pitcher.
pied (m): leg (of furniture).
pinces (f.pl.): pliers.
placard (m): closet, cupboard.
plafond (m): ceiling.
planche à découper (f): chopping board.
planche à repasser (f): ironing board.
plancher (m): floor.
plat (m): serving dish.
plinthe (f): baseboard, plinth.
poignée (f): handle, knob.
porte (f): door.
poubelle (f): trashcan, dustbin.
poutre (f): beam.
prise (f) **de courant**: electric plug.

réchaud (m): hot plate, small stove.
réfrigérateur (m): refrigerator.
robinet (m): faucet, tap.

saladier (m): salad bowl.
serpillière (f): mop.
serviette (f) **de table**: napkin.
serviette éponge (f): towel.
siège (m): seat.
sommier (m): box mattress.
soucoupe (f): saucer.
soupière (f): tureen.

table (f): table.
tabouret (m): stool.
taie (f) **d'oreiller**: pillow slip *or* pillowcase.
tamis (m): sieve.
tasse (f): cup.
théière (f): teapot.
tire-bouchon (m): corkscrew.
tiroir (m): drawer.
toit (m): roof.
torchon (m): dishtowel, dishcloth.
tournevis (m): screwdriver.
traversin (m): bolster.

ventilateur (m): fan, ventilator.
verre (m): drinking glass.
vis (f): screw.
vitre (f): window pane.

LA POSTE

THE POST OFFICE

The official abbreviation is now **P et T, (Postes et Télécom-munications)**; many people, however, still use **PTT (Postes, Télégraphes et Téléphones)**.

accusé (m) **de réception**, 'notice of receipt' of registered letter.
affranchir, 'to put stamps on';
affranchissement (m), 'postage'.
annuaire (m), 'telephone directory'.

bon du trésor (m), 'government bond'.
bottin (m), 'telephone directory'.

cabine téléphonique (f), 'telephone kiosk' (US: 'booth').
caisse d'épargne (f), 'savings bank'.
colis (m), 'parcel'.
compte de chèques postaux (m), abbreviated *CCP*, postal checking account;
  virement (m), payment from one *CCP* to another;
  paiement (m), payment in cash directly from *CCP* to recipient.

destinataire (m), 'addressee' of package, 'to'.

emprunt (m), 'bond issue', 'government loan'.
expéditeur (m), 'sender' of package, 'from'.

facteur (m), 'postman'.

guichet (m), 'window'.

jeton (m), 'token' for telephone.

mandat (m), 'money order';
  émettre un mandat, to issue, send a money order.

paquet (m), 'parcel'.
pli (m), 'envelope', 'cover';
  sous pli séparé, 'under separate cover'.
pneu(matique) (m), 'local express letter'.

récépissé (m), 'receipt of registration'.
recommander, 'to register', 'to send by registered mail'.

télégramme (m), 'telegram'.
timbre (m), 'stamp'.

Post offices are generally open from 8 a.m. to 7 p.m. (*de 8h à 19h sans interruption*) from Monday to Friday, and from 8 a.m. to 4.30 p.m. on Saturday (*de 8h à 16h30 sans interruption*).

SPECTACLES

ENTERTAINMENT

LE CINÉMA
actualités (f. pl.): 'news', 'newsreel'.

court-métrage (m): 'short film', 'short subject'; often *un documentaire*, 'a documentary'.

dessin animé (m): 'animated cartoon'.
distribution (f): 'cast'.

en exclusivité (f): Said of a first-run film, *un film qui passe en exclusivité*.

générique (m): 'credits'.
grand écran (m): 'the cinema'; as opposed to *le petit écran*, 'television'.

metteur en scène (m): 'director'.

ouvreuse (f): the lady who ushers you to your seat; you tip her 10% to 15% of the price of the *séance* (q.v.).

publicité (f): 'advertising.' Amply makes up for the near absence of advertising on French radio and television.

séance (f): 'the show', including *court-métrage, grand film*, and *publicité*.
spectacle permanent (m): 'continuous show', as opposed to, for example, *séance à 15h et à 21h*.

tourner un film: 'to make a film'.

vedette (f): 'star', of either sex.

LE THÉÂTRE
création (f): the first time a play or rôle is directed or performed by a particular person.

entr'acte (m): 'interval' (US: 'intermission').

hymne national (m): 'national anthem'; there is none at a French theatre!, as there is in England immediately after the play.

jeune premier (m): 'young actor in leading role'.

location (f): 'the booking' of seats; *louer*, 'to book'.

pièce (f): 'play'.
place (f): 'seat'.

relâche (f): 'no performance'.
représentation (f): 'performance'.
reprise (f): 'revival' of a play.

souffleur (m): 'prompter'; **souffler**, 'to prompt'.
spectacle (m): 'show'; you do not say '*séance*' in speaking of a play.
Such terms as *distribution, metteur en scène, ouvreuse, publicité* apply as well to the theatre; see above CINÉMA.

LA RADIO, LA TÉLÉVISION (LA TÉLÉ).
chaine (f): 'channel'.

émission (f): 'program'.

haute fidélité (f): 'high fidelity'.

indicatif (m): 'theme music'.
informations (f. pl.): 'news'.

micro(phone) (m): 'microphone'.
modulation de fréquence (f): 'FM'.

ORTF (m): *Office de Radiodiffusion-Télévision Française* ('French National Broadcasting Corporation').

poste (m): 'set' (radio or TV).

réseau (m): 'network'.

speaker (m), **speakerine** (f): 'announcer'.

DISQUES
disque (m): 'record'.

enregistrement (m): 'recording'.

microsillon (m): 'long-playing record'.

plateau (m): 'turntable'.
pochette (f): 'record sleeve', 'cover'.

saphir (m): 'needle'.

trente-trois (33) tours (m): 'long-playing record'.

LE TÉLÉPHONE

THE TELEPHONE

abonné (m): 'subscriber'.
annuaire (m): 'telephone directory'.
appel (m): 'call'.

bottin (m): 'telephone directory'.

cabine (f) **téléphonique**: 'telephone booth'.
communication (f): 'call'.

décrocher: 'to lift' (the receiver off the hook).
donner un coup de téléphone (or **de fil**): 'to make a telephone call', 'to ring up'.

écouteur (m): 'ear-piece', 'receiver'.

faire le numéro: 'to dial the number'.

jeton (m): 'token' for public phone.

ligne (f): 'line'.
ligne résidentielle (f): 'party (shared) line'.

poste (m): 'extension'.

avec préavis pour Untel: 'personal call for (US: person-to-person to) So-and-So'.

raccrocher: 'to hang up', 'ring off'.

standard (m): 'switchboard'.
standardiste (m. *or* f.): 'operator'.

taxiphone (m): 'public telephone', requiring *un jeton*.
tonalité (f): 'dial tone'.

French phones in *cabines publiques*, like some English ones but unlike American ones, have that button which you must press *immediately* after you have heard your party pick up his receiver and answer you. If you don't press it he won't hear you and your 'conversation' will be a monologue.

Le téléphone sonne. 'The phone is ringing.'
Allo, oui? (or *J'écoute*, or *Je vous écoute*). 'Hello, yes?'
Qui est à l'appareil? 'Who's calling?' 'Who is this?'
C'est Monsieur Dupont. Voulez-vous me passer (Je voudrais parler à) Mademoiselle Dumas. 'This is Mr. Dupont. May I speak (I'd like to speak) with Miss Dumas.'
Ici Mademoiselle Dumas (or *C'est elle-même*). 'This is she speaking.'
Monsieur X est occupé sur une autre ligne; ne quittez pas, s'il vous plaît (or *un petit moment*, or *voulez-vous patienter*). 'Mr. X is busy on another line, hold on please.'
Pouvez-vous (puis-je) lui faire la commission? 'Will you (May I) take a message for him (her)?'
A quel numéro peut-on vous rappeler? 'Where can we call you back?'
A quelle heure peut-on le toucher? 'What's the best time to reach him?'
Voulez-vous répéter? Je vous entends mal, il y a du bruit sur la ligne. 'I'm sorry I can't hear you; the line is bad, would you mind repeating?'
Nous avons été coupés. 'We've been cut off.'

A recorded voice may tell you: *Il n'y a pas d'abonné au numéro que vous avez demandé.* 'You've dialled a wrong number (there's no subscriber at this number).'

LA VOITURE

CARS

aile (f): 'mudguard' (US: 'fender').

allée (f): 'avenue', 'drive'. Not an 'alley', which is *passage* (m), *impasse* (f).

amortisseur (m): 'shock absorber'.

arbre à cames (m): 'camshaft'.

auto-route (f) **à péage** (m): 'motorway with toll' (US: 'thruway').

bateau (m): depression in pavement (US: 'sidewalk') in front of *porte-cochère* used as car exit and entrance.

batterie (f): 'battery'.

bougie (f): 'spark   plug'.

break (m): 'estate car', 'shooting brake' (US: 'station wagon').

brûler un feu: 'to go through a red light'.

caler: 'to stall'.

capot (m): 'bonnet' (US: 'hood').

capote (f): the top of a convertible.

caramboler: 'to swerve (US: 'careen') into other cars'.

carambolage (m): 'multiple smashup'.

carrefour (m): 'crossroads'.

carrossable: 'practicable' (a road).

carte-grise (f): official 'registration'.

ceinture de sécurité (f): 'safety belt'.

chaussée (f): 'road surface'.

chaussée deformée (f): 'bad road surface'.

chaussée glissante (f): 'slippery road surface'.

clé (f) **de contact**: 'ignition key'.

clignotant (m): 'indicator', 'turn signal'.

clous (m. pl.): 'zebra crossing' (US: 'crosswalk'); *traverser dans les clous*, 'to cross (the street) at the zebra crossing'. See also *passage clouté*.

coffre (m): 'boot' (US: 'trunk').

collision (f): 'collision'.

conducteur (m): 'driver'.

conduite (f): 'driving'.
   la bonne conduite: 'good driving'; *la mauvaise conduite*: 'bad driving'.

contravention (f): 'fine'. Familiarly, *une contredanse*.

crever: 'to puncture'. *Avoir une crevaison, un pneu crevé*: 'to have a flat tire'.

cric (m): 'jack'.

décapotable (f): 'convertible'.

démarrer: 'to start up'.

déraper: 'to skid'; **dérapage** (m): 'skid'.
déviation (f): 'detour'.
différentiel (m): 'differential'.
direction (f): 'steering'.
disque de stationnement (m): required in the *Zone bleue* (q.v.)
dos d'âne (m): 'hump' in the road.
doubler: 'to overtake' (US: 'pass').

écraser: 'to run over'; **se faire écraser**: 'to be run over'.
embrayage (m): 'clutch'. **embrayer**: 'to let in the clutch';
    débrayer: 'to let out the clutch'.
essence (f): 'petrol' (US: 'gas', 'gasoline'). *Faire le plein*: 'to fill
    up'.
essuie-glaces (m): 'windscreen (windshield) wipers'.

feu (m): 'light'. *Les feux arrière*: 'taillights'.   *Un feu cligno-
    tant*: 'blinking yellow light'. *Les feux de position*: 'parking lights'.
    Les feux de signalisation: 'traffic lights' (*rouge, orange, vert*). *Les
    (feux) stop*: 'brake lights'.
frein (m): 'brake'. *Le frein à main*: 'hand brake'.

galerie (f) **de toit**: 'luggage rack'.
gas-oil (m): 'diesel oil'.
glace (f): 'window'.
graissage (m): 'lubrication'.

huile (f): 'oil'.

impasse (f): 'blind alley', 'dead end', 'cul-de-sac'.

lubrifier: 'to lubricate'.
lunette arrière (f): 'rear window'.

manivelle (f): 'crank'.
motard (m): 'motorcycle (motorway) policeman'.
moteur (m): 'engine'.

panne (f): 'breakdown'. *Tomber en panne*: 'to break down'. *Avoir
    une panne sèche*: 'to run out of gas'.   *La dépanneuse*: 'break-
    down lorry' (US: 'wrecker', 'tow car').
papillon (m): the paper you find on your windshield to tell you
    that you have been fined.
parc automobile (m): the number of cars in a given country.
pare-brise (m): 'windscreen' (US: 'windshield').
parking (m): 'a parking area', 'car-park'.
passage clouté (m): 'zebra crossing' (US: 'crosswalk'. See *clous*).
passage à niveau (m): 'level (grade, railway) crossing'.
permis (m) **de conduire**: 'driving license'.
phare (m): 'headlight'.
plaque minéralogique (f): 'registration (license) plate'.

point mort (m): 'neutral'.
police (f): 'the police'. *Un policier*: 'policeman', 'detective'. *Un agent de police*: 'policeman'. *Monsieur l'Agent* is the polite form of address when you ask directions etc.
police (f) **d'assurance**: 'insurance policy'.
pompiste (m): 'attendant' in filling station.
pont (m): 'bridge'.
pont arrière (m): 'rear axle'.
portière (f): 'car door'.
poste (m) **d'essence**: 'filling (petrol, gas) station'.
pot d'échappement (m): 'exhaust pipe'.

queue de poisson, faire une: to cut too sharply in front of another driver.

réservoir (m) **d'essence**: 'gas tank'.
rétroviseur (m): 'rearview mirror'.
rodage, en: 'running in' (US: 'breaking in').
rond-point (m): 'roundabout' (US: 'traffic circle').
route (f): 'road' (US: 'highway').
rue (f): 'street'.

sens (m): 'direction'. *Sens giratoire*: 'roundabout', 'traffic island'. *Sens interdit*: 'no entry', *Sens obligatoire*: 'compulsory direction'. *Sens unique*: 'one-way'.
soupape (f): 'valve'.
stationnement (m): 'parking'.

tableau de bord (m): 'instrument panel', 'dashboard'.
tambour de frein (m): 'brake drum'.
tonneau, faire un: 'to overturn'.
trottoir (m): 'pavement' (US: 'sidewalk').

verglas (m): 'sheet ice' on road.
vitesse (f): 'speed'; also, 'gear'. *La boîte de vitesses*: 'gearbox'. *En première*: 'in first gear'. *En seconde*: 'in second gear'. *En troisième*: 'in third gear'. *En quatrième*: 'in fourth gear'. *Passer les vitesses*: 'to change gears'. *Etre au point mort*: 'to be in neutral'. *Faire marche arrière*: 'to back up'. *Reculer*: 'to back up'. *Mettre en marche arrière*: 'to go into reverse'.
volant (m): 'steering wheel'.

zone bleue (f): area in which you may park for a limited time or only on certain days of the month. The *disque de stationnement* must be placed on the windshield to show when you arrived and when you should leave.

ENGLISH—FRENCH

Cross-reference Index

N. B. This might better be termed a 'mere' cross-reference index, so as to give you a more accurate idea of its completeness, reliability and usefulness. The French word given after each English entry is meant as a suggestion of where to turn in the main French-English text; it may not even be the translation of the English word, or the only translation possible. Where more than one French word is given, you will want to look each of them up in the main French-English text, to find which one suits which situation. And indeed, a number of items in the main text have not been cross-referenced here, because they do not lend themselves to the distorted condensation which an index necessitates.

able: habile
absent-mindedness: distraire, se
about to, to be: point
accelerator: champignon
according to: d'après
acquit, to: innocenter
actor: comédien
adapted from: d'après
adjoining: attenant
administration: direction
administrator: cadre
adult: personne
advantageous: intéressé, intérêt
affair: affaire, bricole, liaison
against: moyennant
agreement: accord, entendre parler
aid: concours
airport: gare
alcohol: boisson
all aboard: abordable
all right: accord, ça va, entendre parler
All Saints' Day: Toussaint
almond: dragée
already: déjà
also: aussi
alter: truc
alteration: retouche

always: toujours
amiable: abordable
amusement: distraire, se
and so on: avenant
announcement: faire-part
annoy, to: chiffon, tiquer
antiques: antiquité
antiquity: antiquité
anyhow: façon, toujours
apparatus: appareil
apparently: conditionnel
appeal, to: appel, chanter
appear, to: produire, se
apprenticeship: stage
approachable: abordable
approve, to: agréer
apron: chemise
argue, to: discuter
aroma: bouquet
arrange, to: arranger, mettre
arrive: arriver
article: article
artist: interprète
ashtray: feu
as is: tel quel
ask, to: pose
asparagus: asparagus, asperge
astonishing: invraisemblable
at bottom: fond
attempt, to: expérience
at the time: coup

attract, to: attirer
attraction: attrayant, clou
attractive: attrayant, séduire
auction: bougie
avail oneself of, to: emprunt
awareness: prise

bachelor: garçon
back: dossier, fond
background: fond
bacon: bacon
bad temper: mouvement d'humeur
baggage: bagage
bald: cheveux
ball-point pen: bic, bureau
bang bang!: pan pan pan!
bank note: billet
bargain: affaire, marché
barracks: chambre
basically: foncièrement
bathe, to: nager
bather: baigneur
bathrobe: chemise
battery: pile
beat, to: dérouiller
because: si
bedroom: chambre
beer: demi
begin, to: mettre
beginner: débutant
believe: tenir
benefit: bénéfice
beside the point: voir
beyond: au-delà
billion: billion
birthday: fête
biscuit: gâteau
bit: bout
bitch: garce
black coffee: crème
blackmail: chanter
Black Maria: salade
blame, to: donner
bleach: Javel, eau de
blend: marier
blister: ampoule
block of houses: pâté maison
blouse: bonneterie, chemise

blue, to be: bleu
blues: bleu
blunder: gaffe, pied
boat hook: gaffe
bolster: traversin
bone: arête
bootblack: cireur
borrow, to: emprunt
boss: patron
bother, to: déranger, peine, tracasser, travailler
bottle: consigne, flacon
bouquet: bouquet
bow tie: papillon
boxing: box
boy: garçon
boy friend: petit(e) ami(e)
branch store: brancher
brand name: marque
brass instruments: cuivres
bread: pain
breadcrumbs: chapeau
breakdown: dépanner, dépression
breeding: correct, éducation, élever
bribe: bribes, pot
bristle: cheveux
bruise: bleu
brush, to: brosser
buckle down, to: mettre
bunch: marché
burdened: grève
bus: car
business: affaire, boîte, histoire
businessman: affaire, capitaine d'industrie
bustle, to: affaire
busy: chargé, occuper
butterfly: papillon

Cabinet: cabinets
cake: cake, galette, gâteau, pain
call: appel, coup
calm: tranquille
camera: appareil
camping, to go: camper
candle: bougie, chandelle

candlestick: ampoule
car: car
caravan: caravane
carbon copy: double
care about, to: tenir
carelessly: au diable, habillé
car-park: parc
carpeting: maquette, tapis
carton: cartouche
cartridge: cartouche
case: cas, housse
-case-: porte-
casual dress: habillé
catastrophe: sinistre
catch: catch, coincer
cat food: pâté maison
cavity: carie
celebrate, to: arroser, fête
cell: cellule
chance: chance, occasion
chandelier: ampoule
change: appoint, dépayser, monnaie
character: caractère
charm: cachet
cheap: donner
cheap wine: bleu
chest of drawers: dresser
child: rejeton
chill: coup, frapper
chisel: ciseau
chord: corde
chubby: rondelet(te)
church: temple
cigarette case: feu
cigarette lighter: feu
clarify: tirer
class: classe
classroom: classe
clause: avenant
clean: étanche, propre
clever: astuce, habile, savant
cloakroom: consigne
close: tirer
clothes: confection, dresser
coach: car
coal: bougnat
cold: froid
color-blind: daltonien
comb, to: coup

comedy: comédien
come in: Entrez !
coming: arriver
comma: virgule
commuter: banlieue
competition: concours
complain, to: rouspéter
compulsory: obligatoire
conclusion: tirer
conduct, to: conduire, direction
conductor: conduire
confectionery: confection
congratulations: chapeau
connection: piston, rapporter, relations
consent: agréer
conservative: conserver
consider, to: interroger, s'
continue, to: poursuivre, se; suivre
convenient: commode
cook: fourneau
cord: corde
correct: correct, reprendre
cost, to: chercher, rente
counter: zinc
country: bleu, pays
cracked: toqué
cracker: gâteau
craftsman: artisanat
credit: avoir, passif
crew-necked: ras du cou
crisis: crise
crowd: monde
crude: crudités
cuff: manchette
curate: curé
curator: conserver
cure: cure
curtain: rideau

dam: barrage
dance: boom
dance attendance, to: pied
debit: passif
deceive: tromper
decimal point: virgule
decree: arrêté
defrost: dégivrer

degree: diplôme
deliberately: exprès
department store: boutique
departure: partance
deposit: appointements, arrhes, consigne
depression: dépression
deranged: déranger
desk: bureau
deviation: entorse
develop, to: mettre en valeur
devil, to the: au diable
did he?: n'est-ce pas?
didn't he?: n'est-ce pas?
die, to: crever
difficult: donner
direct, to: conduire
direction: direction, indiquer, sens
disappear: filer
disappoint: tromper
discount: remise
discuss, to: discuter
dishonest: bleu
dish rack: égout
dismiss, to: congé
disservice: desservir
distance: au diable, bout
divorce, to: divorcer
do it yourself: bricole
doll: baigneur
dormitory: chambre
doormat: bassin
double: double
do without, to: passer
drain board: bassin, égout
draw up, to: dresser
dredge, to: draguer
dress, to: dresser
dressing gown: chemise
dressy: habillé
drink: boisson, consommation, pot
drip: goûter
drive, to: conduire
drop: goûter
drop in, to: passer
drop off, to: déposer
drunk: bleu
drunkenness: intoxication

dub, to: double
dunce: chameau
dupe: fait, avoir
dust: chiffon, poussière
dustbin: boîte

ear piece: écouteur
easy: gâteau
education: éducation
egg: œuf
eke out, to: arrondir
Eldorado: Pérou
electrician: plomb
electric switch: interrupteur
electric torch: ampoule
embarrass: embarrasser, peine
encore: encore
encumber, to: embarrasser
end: bout
endlessly: vue
enhance, to: mettre en valeur
enlarge, to: agrandir
enlightened: évolué, illuminé
enough: assez
errand boy: garçon
escape: échapper
every time: coup
exactly: juste
examination: concours, examen, passer, professeur
exceptional: extra
excitement: émotion
exhausted: abruti, bout, claque, crever, linge
experience: expérience
experiment: expérience
expiration: échéance
explode, to: sauter
extra: en plus, en sus, extra
eyesight: presbyte, vue

failure: échéance, four
fall due, to: échéance
fall through, to: tomber
far-fetched: cheveux
farm: ferme
farsighted: presbyte
fashion: façon
fat: graisse

fat content: graisse, maigre
favor: service
fed up, to be: assez
feel well, to: forme
fees: appointements
fellow guest: bourratif
fiddlesticks!: fariboles
figurative: figuratif
figure of speech: figuratif
file: classe, dossier
filling: bourratif, carie
filthy: infect
find: astuce, tomber, trouvaille
fire: feu, incendie
firm: ferme, maison, S.A.
first draft: jet
first of all: abordable
fix, to: arranger
flag: tricolore
flask: flacon
flat: bémol
flat tire: crever
floodlighting: illuminé
flop: claque, four, navet
follow, to: suivre
fool, to: avoir
foot: pied
forgive, to: passer
former: jeunes, les
forward, to: suivre
form: forme
fountain: jet
fourth: quart
frame: cadre
franc: franc
frank: carré, franc
freckle: roux (rousse)
free, to: affranchir
freezer: congélateur
French leave: filer
frog in the throat: chameau
front page: une
fruitcake: cake
frying pan: poêle
full: complet, plein
fun, to have: distraire, se
funds: crédit
furnace: fourneau
fuse: brancher, plomb
fuss: histoire, monde

gain weight, to: grossir
gap: lacune
garage: box, garage
garlic: marché
gender: genre
get rid of, to: sauter
girdle: bonneterie
girl: fille
girl friend: fille, petit(e) ami(e)
give back, to: rendre
glance: coup
go, to: marcher, rendre; sauver, se
go home, to: maison
goldfish: poisson rouge
good: sage
good luck!: chance, professeur
go on!: aller
got it!: ça y est
graduate, to: diplôme
grandson: petit-fils
grease: graisse
greengrocer: asparagus
grind, to: moudre
grumpy: grognon
guff: histoire
guilty: coupable

hair: cheveux
hand: coup, passer
handkerchief: pochette
handy: commode
happen, to: arriver; produire, se
hard up: embarrasser
harm: mal
hat: chapeau
have to, to: falloir
headline: manchette
headquarters: siège
heads or tails: pile
healer: cure
hear of, to: entendre parler
heart attack: crise
heat, to: feu
heckle, to: chahuter
height: taille
help: arranger, concours, coup, dépanner, jouer, servir
helping: portion

hint: truc, tuyau
history: histoire
hoax, to: boîte
-holder: porte-
holiday: congé, férié, fermeture annuelle, fête, pont
home: maison
honeyed: mielleux
hoodwink, to: donner
hopeless: issue, tirer
hostel: auberge
hot air: baratin, boniment
house: maison
how . . . !: ce que, que
how . . . ?: comment
how are you?: ça va
humor: mouvement d'humeur
hungry, to make: donner
hurt: bobo, froisser, mal, peine
hypnotize, to: aimant
hysterics: crise

if: si
if only: que
ignore: ignorer
ill: souffrant
illegal trade: circulation
imagine, to: figurer, se
imminent: prochain
implicate, to: mettre
implied: entendre parler
import, to: importer
important: important, importer
impressive: important, impression
impulse: coup
in addition: en plus, en sus, extra
Inc.: S.A.
incidentals: faux frais
included: en plus
income: rente
in exchange for: moyennant
infected: infect
influence: crédit, influer sur, jouer, piston
informal: sans façon

-in-law: parent
inn: auberge
in order: règlement
in other words: autrement
in pain: mal
insert, to: présenter
inside out: sens dessus-dessous
installation: pose
instantaneous: instantané
interest: intérêt
interpreter: interprète
interurban trains: ligne
in the long run: échéance
in the midst of: plein
in the neighborhood: parages
in theory: en principe
in touch with: liaison
introduce, to: présenter
in trouble: auberge, bêtise
iron: coup, jeannette
ironmonger: couleurs, marchand de
issue: issue

jacket: pochette, tailleur
jam: embouteillage
jar: pot
joke: blague, farces et attrapes
jumper: bonneterie
just: juste
juvenile delinquent: blouson noir

keep, to: tenir
kitchen utensils: pile
knock: frapper, toc
knocked out: chandelle
know, to: figurer, se; savoir
knowledge: bagage

labor: travailler
lack: manquer
lamp: ampoule
last straw: manquer
laundry: linge
lavatory: cabinets, lavabo, quelque part
law: droit

lay out, to: mettre
lazy: cheveux, fumiste
lead, to: conduire
leave: congé, déposer
left: droit
lemonade: limonade
lend, to: emprunt, passer
let out, to: reprendre
letter opener: coupe-papier
lettuce: salade
liable: passible
license: licencié, vignette
licentious: licencié
lift: ascenseur
light: feu, illuminé
light bulb: ampoule
light meter: cellule
lime: limonade
line, to: double
linen: linge
literal: figuratif, pied
loaded: chargé, recharge
loaf: pain
loan: emprunt
look: air
look for, to: chercher
loose talk: baratin, boniment
lose weight, to: grossir
lost, to be: nager
lotion: embrocation
love affair: liaison
love, to: raffoler
Ltd.: S.A.

machine: appareil
magnet: aimant
maiden name: fille
main thing: essentiel
major: bémol
make believe, to: semblant
malicious: malicieux
man: garçon
manage, to: arriver, débrouiller, se; tirer
manila folder: chemise
manner: façon, genre
march: marcher
mark: marque
market: marché, marcher
marry: marier

match: feu
match book: pochette
matter: affaire
may I?: permettre
meager: maigre
meaning: sens
medical exam.: visite
medium size: patron
merger: fusionner
mess: gâchis, salade
meter: compteur
metric system: mètre
midwife: sage
mimeograph: ronéotyper
miner: bémol
minor: bémol
mint, to: frapper
mischievous: malicieux
miss, to: manquer
mistake: tromper
model: mannequin
mold, to: moudre
money: galette, monnaie
mood: mouvement d'humeur
mop: serpellière
move, to: bouger, émotion
much more: autrement
mushroom: champignon
musical score: partition
mussel: moudre
must: falloir

nail: clou
narcotics squad: monde
National Lottery: dixième
nausea: mal
nearly: manquer, quasiment
nearsighted: presbyte
near thing: juste
necessarily: forcément, obligatoire
negligee: habillé
neighborhood: quartier
neither: non plus
newspaper: papier
New Year: étrennes, réveillon
next: prochain
nibble: bout
night club: boîte
nightgown: chemise

nobody: personne
no joke!: blague
no matter how, when etc.: importer
northern: méridional
not bad: mal, pas mal
note: billet
notice: licencié
not know, to: ignorer
not likely: invraisemblable, passible
no use: peine
nuisance: intoxication
number plate: plaque minéralogique
nun: religieuse

observe, to: constater
obstacle: embarrasser
obvious: sauter
of course: entendre parler
offend, to: froisser
office: bureau, cabinets, maison
OK: accord, ça va
older generation: jeunes, les
old maid: fille
on behalf of: part
one another: une
only: que
on purpose: exprès
opinion: prise
otherwise: autrement
ouch!: aïe!
outbid, to: surenchérir
outlaw: droit
outline, to: brosser, ligne
out of place: cheveux
outspoken: franc
oven: four
overall: bleu, combinaison
overheat, to: griller
overlook, to: échapper
overtake, to: double
owe, to: chandelle
own: propre
pain: peine, souffrant
pan: casserole
panic, to: raffoler
paper: papier

paper handkerchief: jeter
parent: parent
park: parc
park, to: garer, se
parking fine: papillon
partition: partition
party: boom, réveillon
pass, to: croiser
passive voice: passif
patch, to: rafistoler
pattern: patron
pavement: pavés
paving blocks: pavés
pawn, to: clou, mont-de-piété
pawnshop: mont-de-piété
pay attention, to: gaffe
payment: appointements, règlement, verser
people: gens, monde
percussion instruments: cuivres, pile
perfect, to: point
person: personne
pheasant: faisan
pick up, to: chercher, reprendre
pile: marché, pile
pillar box: boîte
pillow: traversin
pipe: tuyau
pipestem: fourneau
playground: jeunes, les
play pen: parc
pleasure: agréer
plot: combinaison
plug: brancher, prise
plumber: plomb
point, to: point
point out, to: signaler
poised: pose
poisoning: intoxication
polish: cireur, dérouiller
polite: correct, élever
pocket: pochette
pool: bassin
portion: part
post bills, to: afficher
postman: étrennes
postmark: cachet
postpone, to: remise

pot luck: pot
pour, to: verser
practical joke: farces et attrapes
practically: quasiment
prejudice: prévention
presbytery: presbyte
prescription: vignette
preserve, to: conserver
pretend, to: semblant
prevention: prévention
priceless: impayable
primary: primordial
print, to: impression
private: particulier
probably: invraisemblable
problem: crise
professor: professeur
profit: bénéfice, intérêt, rapporter
propriety: propre
province: province
punctuation: ponctuation
puncture: crever

quarter: quart, quartier
question: pose
quite a lot: pas mal
-rack: porte-
radio v. **wireless**
rain: flotter
raincoat: étanche
rank: classe
rather: assez
raw vegetables: crudités
ready-made clothes: confection
realize: rendre
reception: vin d'honneur
recommend, to: indiquer, recommander
reconcile: rapprocher
record, to: magnétophone
record player: électrophone
red-haired: roux (rousse)
reduction: hausse
refill: recharge
refined: évolué
reflect, to: réfléchir
refrigerator: congélateur

regards to: manquer
region: pays
register: inscrire, s'; recommander
regulation: règlement
relative: parent, petit-fils
reluctantly: à contre-cœur
reminder: pense-bête
rent: rente
repair, to: arranger, dépanner
reporter: rapporter
reproach: rapprocher
resign, to: licencié
restless: bouger
restore, to: mettre
result: donner
retirement: retraite
retreat: retraite
return ticket: aller
reverse: marcher
ride: tour, faire un
right: correct, donner, droit
right moment: tomber
right-thinking: penser
ripe: fait
rise: hausse
risk: risquer
road block: barrage
room: chambre, espace
rot, to: moisir
rude: élever
rug: tapis
rule: règlement
ruler: mètre
run, to: filer, marcher
run into, to: croiser

sack, to: licencié
sadness: chagrin
saint's day: fête
salad: salade
salad dressing: dresser
salary: appointements, traitement
sales: appointements
sandwich: sandwich
sausage: saucisse
scale model: mannequin, maquette
scalp: cheveux

scholar: savant
science fiction: anticipation
scientist: savant
scissors: ciseau
scour, to: récurer
scraps: bribes, bout
season, to: saison, la belle
seat: espace, siège, strapontin
secondhand: occasion
seduce, to: séduire
seem, to: air
seize, to: saisir
select: sélectionner
self-interested: intéressé
sense: sens
servant: domestique
serve, to: desservir
serves you right: chercher, pied
set fire, to: feu
set to music, to: mettre
sewer: égout
shark: faisan
sharp: bémol
shirt: chemise
shirtmaker: chemise
shirtsleeves, in: chemise
shop: boutique
shore: grève
shorthand: dactylo
shorts: pantalon
show up, to: point
shrink: bouger
shrug: hausse
sin, to: falloir
sincerely: sans façon
sing, to: chanter
single: double
single ticket: aller
size: patron, taille
sizeable: important
skilful: habile
skimmed: maigre
slacks: bonneterie
slam, to: claque
slap: claque
sleep tight: bobo
slip: combinaison
slip, to let: échapper

slipcover: housse
smallness: petitesse
small town: pays
smock: chemise
snack: cas, goûter
snap: fermeture éclair
snapshot: instantané
snuff box: tabatière
So-and-So: un tel
soap flakes: linge
something: quelque chose
somewhere: quelque part
son-in-law: gendre
sort, to: sélectionner
sort of, a: genre
so-so: quelconque
sound: valide
southern: méridional
space: espace
split hairs, to: cheveux
spoil, to: gâteau
spotty: lacune
sprain: entorse
sprinkle, to: asperge
square: espace, parc, terre-plein
stage: stage
stamp, to: affranchir
start, to: démarrer, mettre
station: gare
steering: direction
step: marcher
step-: parent
stingy: radin
stockings: bonneterie
stomach ache: mal
story: histoire
stove: fourneau, poêle
straw mattress: bassin
stretch, to: allonger
strike: frapper, grève
strikebreaker: bleu
striking: saisir
string bag: marché
stringed instruments: cuivres
strongbox: coffre-fort
stubborn: volontaire
stuck, to be: coincer
study: pencher, se

stuffing: farces et attrapes
stupid: abruti, chameau
suburbs: banlieue, faubourg, ligne
succeed, to: marcher
such and such: tant, tel ou tel
suit: complet, tailleur
summarize: dresser
summer: saison, la belle
sum up, to: point
sunburn: coup
superfluous: double, extra
supposed to: conditionnel, en principe
surrender: rendre
swaddling clothes: langes
swear word: gros mot
sweater: bonneterie
sweep, to: coup, fumiste
sweetheart: petit(e) ami(e)
swim, to: nager
swimming pool: nager
swimsuit: bonneterie, nager
system: système

table of contents: table des matières
tablet: bureau, cachet
take care of, to: occuper, suivre
take in, to: reprendre
taken in, to be: avoir, bleu, marcher
talkative: intarissable
talk shop, to: boutique
taper: bougie
tape recorder: magnétophone
taste, to: goûter
tea: goûter
teacher: professeur
telephone: appareil
television: radio
temperament: caractère
tenth: dixième
terminal: gare
that is: c'est-à-dire
that's the end!: bouquet
thaw: dégivrer
theme song: indicatif
there!: aller, ça y est, toc

therefore: aussi
thin: maigre
thingumabob: machin, truc
think, to: penser
thumb one's nose, to: pied
ticket: billet, espace, siège
tie: papillon
tight: juste
till, to: travailler
tin: boîte
tip: étrennes, pourboire, service, truc, tuyau
toast: griller, pain
tobacco: tabac
tobacconist's: jeton, tabac
tobacco pouch: blague
token: jeton
tomboy: garce
too bad: pot
tool shed: remise
toothpick: cure-dent
towel: gant de toilette
tower: tour, faire un
town house: hôtel particulier
track down, to: dépister
traffic: circulation
traffic jam: embouteillage
traffic light: feu
tragedy: comédien
train, to: dresser, stage
translate, to: rendre
translation: professeur
transparency: diapositive
treatment: traitement
trick: tour, faire un
trinket: bibelot
trouble: histoire, intoxication, mal
trouble, to go to: donner, mal, peine
troublesome: donner
trousers: pantalon
turnip: navet
turtle-necked: ras du cou
typewriter: dactylo
typist: dactylo

under: sous
underpants: combinaison
undershirt: chemise

understand: saisir, suivre
unfaithful: tromper
unjust: juste
upholstery: tapis
upset: émotion, retourner
upside-down: sens dessus-dessous
useful: service, servir

valid: valable
validate, to: valide
valuable: valable
vendor: marché
vicar: curé
victim: sinistre
view: vue
visionary: illuminé
visit: visite
voluntary: volontaire
vomit: rendre

wages: appointements
waist: taille
wait and see: voir
waiter: garçon
walk, to: marcher; tour, faire un
wallpaper: tapis
warm, to: chambre
washbasin: bassin
washcloth: gant de toilette
washing: linge
washstand: lavabo
watch out: gare
water, to: arroser
waterproof: étanche
watertight: étanche
wax, to: cireur
wear, to: mettre
wedding: marier
weight: marché
well . . . : enfin
well! comment, tenir
well qualified: calé, corde

what: quoi
what'shisname: machin, truc
what of it?: encore
which: quoi
while we're at it: tant
whimsical: farfelu
white coffee: crème
window: tabatière
window-shopping: lèche-vitrines
wireless: électrophone, radio
wise: sage
with: avec
with difficulty: difficilement
without: avec
woman: fille
wonder, to: demander, se; interroger, s'
woodwinds: cuivres
work: pain
work, to: marcher, pied, travailler
worldly: monde
worry, to: en; tracasser, se
worthwhile: valable
wound, to: froisser
wrestling: catch
wrinkle, to: chiffon, froisser
wrong: droit, tromper

X-ray: radio

yawn, to: mettre
yes: oui, si
you: tutoyer
You Know Who: Qui Vous Savez
younger generation: jeunes, les
you're welcome: quoi
youth hostel: auberge

zipper: fermeture éclair